Short Stories for Today

Longman Study Texts

General editor: Richard Adams

Titles in the series:

Short Stories for Today

edited by
Michael Marland

Headmaster, North Westminster Community
School; Honorary Professor of Education,
Warwick University

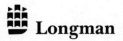

LONGMAN GROUP LIMITED
Longman House
*Burnt Mill, Harlow, Essex CM20 2JE, England
and associated companies throughout the world.*

© Longman Group Limited 1984

First published 1984

ISBN 0 582 33145 5

Set in 10/12pt Linotron Baskerville

*Printed in Hong Kong
by Wilture Printing Co., Ltd.*

Cover illustration by Jane Taylor

Contents

Introduction

The short story today

The range, richness, depth, and human perception of short stories written by British writers in the last twenty-five years is impressive and exciting. To guarantee a keen and intelligent reader a good read, any one of two dozen writers' collections of short stories could be taken from the shelves. Indeed, the overall strength of the short story today is such that it challenges the great periods of English literature: the nineteenth-century novel, romantic poetry, the satire of the Augustan period, or even Elizabethan drama. Such claims may seem excessive enthusiasm for a form little discussed by academics in British universities, and having such an apparently modest position in 'Literature': 'You can read short stories in magazines and newspapers; you can hear them read on the radio! How can they be important?' Yet the range of excellent authors writing now, the seriousness of their themes, and the skill of their writing supports the strongest claims. Indeed, it is almost as if the comparative ease with which the short story can find an audience has opened the form to writers and themes denied to the more costly publishing of the novel, the audience-dependent drama, the regrettably off-the-beaten track poetry, and the popularity-demanding television drama. So we have a tremendous flowering of feminist writing, an exploration of racial themes, many perspectives on growing up, a good representation of black writers, studies of sexuality, a frequent political focus, and many very personal and intense pieces of writing that could probably not have seen the light of day in other more constrained forms.

The very words 'short' and 'story' sound unimpressive, and it is easy to think of the short story as a simple, unimportant literary form of no great weight. Compared with 'the novel', 'drama', or 'poetry', the word 'story' suggests we are dealing

with just a casual, minor telling of a curious episode. The use
of 'short' is odd, and makes the writing sound half-hearted and
trivial. We do not talk about a short song or a short play. To
talk about a 'short story' half suggests that *real* ones are longer.
This is very misleading. Many of our greatest writers have
written at their very best in short stories: Henry James, Joseph
Conrad, D. H. Lawrence, E. M. Forster, Elizabeth Bowen,
Angus Wilson, John Wain, Doris Lessing, Alan Sillitoe – to name
but a few. There are also writers of significance for whom the
short story has been their main or only form: Katherine Mansfield (1882–1923), A. E. Coppard (1878–1957), V. S. Pritchett
(1900–). The last, for instance, is known almost entirely by
his stories, and yet he has been described by the critic Frank
Kermode as 'by such a margin the finest English writer alive
that it hardly seems worth saying so'. The achievement of the
modern short story is immense.

Between the wars and even throughout the Second World
War, stories were often first published in literary magazines or
the intellectual weeklies. In the years represented in this collection, this primary opening for stories has largely ended, and
writers often complain that it is hard to get their stories
published. Yet the flow has continued. BBC radio has been an
encouragement, and some authors (including Stan Barstow)
have had a great deal of encouragement from radio readings.
The collected volumes still come out, and wide-selling paper-
back reprints have brought most of the authors in this collection
to a wide readership. As V. S. Pritchett says, 'Although the
short story is said to have lost its popularity, this is not my
experience: thousands of addicts still delight in it because it is
above all memorable and is not simply read, but re-read again
and again. It is the glancing form of fiction that seems to be
right for the nervousness and restlessness of contemporary life.'[1]

Apart from single-author collections there have been three
important series of anthologies making short stories available
for the thoughtful reader: *Penguin Modern Short Stories*, published
quarterly between 1969 and 1972: the Arts Council's *New Stories*,

published annually since 1977; and *Winter's Tales*, published annually for the last 25 years.

There is one very popular form in which, in a way, the short story is having a new revival: the television play. There have been many dramatizations of existing stories, including Nadine Gordimer's 'Country Lovers' from this volume. Stories by authors such as D. H. Lawrence, H. E. Bates and Roald Dahl have made a subtle and powerful impact on television. But more than that the television *play*, whether in a series or one-off, is very similar to a short story. It too concentrates on a small group of characters, and has to find a single main incident to explore them. Many of the best television playwrights could have written their material in short-story form.

Although it is rarely that a single short story achieves the widespread impact of a play or novel, it is true to say that the short story is a dominant literary form of great interest today.

What is a short story?

Labels do not matter very much, and we have got used to the inadequate tag 'short story'. The term is not primarily concerned with length; indeed a few of the longer 'short stories' are as long as a few of the shorter 'novels'. Rather, 'it is this sense we have of the short story being rooted in a single incident or perception that principally differentiates it from the novel', as the critic Walter Allen puts it.[2] This rooting 'in a single incident' usually leads to a unity of mood and feeling as well, whereas the novel usually thrives on variety. V. S. Pritchett used to write novels, but he describes how he came to change:

> I laboured at novels – two had some success and are still in print – but I was really attracted to concision, intensity, reducing possible novels to essentials. I love the intricacy of the short form, the speed with which it can change from scene to scene. I have always thought that the writer of short stories

is a mixture of reporter, aphoristic wit, moralist and poet – though not 'poetical'; he is something of a ballad-maker, and in the intricacy of his design is close to the writer of sonnets. He has to catch our attention at once, to get the opening line right.[3]

Some student readers find many short stories frustrating because it appears 'nothing very much happens'. Although I have compared television plays with short stories, most television serials and series, especially the popular crime ones, are built around 'action': we are conditioned to expect things to happen, and there to be a climax towards the end, with a quick, sudden final sorting out. These plays hold their audiences (who at all costs must be kept from switching to another channel!) by creating a story-thread of 'what happens next?' The writer of serious short stories often includes incidents, and some of them are dramatic events, like the accident in 'A Time to Keep' or the burning of the hut in 'The Second Hut'. In others the events are important, but because of their ordinariness less dramatic, such as the taking away of the boy in Susan Hill's 'The Custodian' or the domestic tension in 'The Heart'.

Writers who use the short story as a literary form to explore life are more concerned with the *people* than the happenings. Their starting point is to consider why people are as they are, what makes them change, and how they feel. Thus in many stories the big event happens only on the sidelines, whilst we are asked to feel with the people.

A famous Irish writer of short stories, Sean O'Faolain, has expressed this difference between the conventional 'story of action' and the serious modern short story in this analysis:

The modern storyteller, then, has not dispensed with incident or anecdote or plot and all its concomitants, but he has changed their nature. There is still adventure; but it is now an adventure of the mind. There is suspense, and plenty of it, but it is no longer the surprise of a man who opens a door and finds that a corpse falls out, but the surprise of a man who opens a cupboard and finds that a skeleton falls out. There is a climax, but it is not the climax of a woman who discovers her lost jewels in the hatbox but the climax of the woman who discovers her lost happiness in a memory. There is contrivance, but it is not the contrivance of the gangster who deceives his enemy, but of the citizen who deceives his friend.

Usually the writer focuses on a single incident, taking a grab, as it were, at a section of someone's life and holding it up to show through it the whole. Often what could have been for some writers just a simple account of a snippet of life is revealed as an *image*. Just as a painter or a photographer selects a certain view or object and so presents it to us that we see not only it, but see it as standing for whole aspects of life, so the key moment in a great short story has that wider meaning. In Alan Sillitoe's 'A Time to Keep' that image is slipped into a sentence that started by being about something else (page 132):

He couldn't say who was tired most: him, Raymond, or the man whom Raymond's dumper truck knocked flying over the almost sheer slope.

In V. S. Pritchett's story 'The Saint' the moment is comic, as Mr Timberlake is left hanging above the water (page 111):

The boat went on, I saw Mr Timberlake's boots leave the stern as he took an unthoughtful step backwards. He made a last-minute grasp at a stronger and higher branch, and then there he hung a yard above the water, round as a blue damson that is ripe and ready, waiting only for a touch to make it fall.

Perhaps some of the stories have more than one key image – when, for instance, is the old man's deep desolation at losing the boy most powerfully evoked in Susan Hill's 'The Custodian'? But generally one can say that a single moment, or at most a short sequence, is made into a powerful image with significance not only for those characters but for the whole of human life.

A good short-story writer is not merely giving a skilful and well-shaped account of an anecdote; he or she is also drawing out the implications of 'what happens' in the sense of the story, and allowing us to perceive 'what happens' in terms of human feelings, responses and changes. You can answer the question 'what is the story about?' in two ways: one is to recount what happens, the plot; the other is to describe the ideas, what we call 'the theme'. This cannot usually be expressed in a brief, simple summary, but each of the incidents or happenings in these stories has interested the author essentially because of its implications. By the way it is presented, the event is made to reveal wider ideas. For instance, even the private domestic tension of 'The Heart' is so written as to make us ponder the ways in which people impose their will and can be insensitive to the real needs of others.

The short story is infinitely varied, but always has a single close focus that gives it immense power.

The roots of today's short stories

Tales have been told since the earliest human times, and in societies in which the printed form is not readily available because of lack of technology or because of poverty, or in which reading is not universal, or there is inadequate artificial light or leisure to enjoy reading at home, the spoken story has always been the major art form for most people. 'Tale' means something spoken, and the word itself derives from an older word actually meaning 'speech'. A tale is a story told aloud to hold the attention of the audience listening then and there.

Some of the ancient spoken tales have been preserved for us in, for instance, the *Arabian Nights Entertainments*, a collection of stories supposed to have been told by Scheherazade in ancient Egypt, which were collected by an Egyptian storyteller in about the fifteenth century. In Italy in the fourteenth century, Giovanni Boccaccio wrote a series of tales called the *Decameron* (the stories of many of which have been borrowed by English writers, including Shakespeare, Chaucer, Dryden and Keats). The oral tale has always flourished, and has been kept alive where conditions prevent widespread literacy, as in India, the Gaelic-speaking west of Ireland, South America and tribal Africa.

We get a vivid picture, for instance, of storytelling in Gaelic-speaking Ireland at the turn of the century from J. M. Synge, the Irish playwright. He left sophisticated Paris in search of the speech and the stories of the Aran Isles. He met an old half-blind Gaelic speaker, who became his teacher, and from him Synge heard many of the old Irish stories:

> After a while I heard a shuffling on the stairs, and the old dark man I had spoken to in the morning groped his way into the room. I brought him over to the fire, and we talked for many hours.
>
> As we talked he sat huddled together over the fire, shaking and blind, yet his face was indescribably pliant, lighting up with an ecstasy of humour when he told me anything that had a point of wit or malice, and growing sombre and desolate again when he spoke of religion or the fairies.

This oral tradition of storytelling lingers in families, pubs and meetings all over the world. Some writers make this relationship between the literary printed short story and the old oral tradition very clear. Alan Sillitoe, for instance, whose story 'A Time to Keep' is in this collection, wrote:

> The ideal story, I have always felt, is a narrative spoken aloud by an illiterate man to a group surrounding a fire in the forest

at night, or told by a man to his friends in a pub, or at the table during dinner hour in a canteen. I see such a story not as an incident which begins as point A and goes in a line thinly but straight to point B, but rather as a circuitous embellishment, twisting and convoluted, meandering all over the place until, near the end, these irrelevancies can at last be seen to have a point, and so can now come together on the main theme and climax. . . .

The story comes from those who crowd around bench or camp fire or street corner to listen, who move on to fresh pastures, or go back to work, or to a new town because they are harried by persecutions, and don't have much time to listen or, if they do, have not yet got into the habit or fields of literacy that will allow them to absorb novels.

Another distinguished British short-story writer, Sid Chaplin (not represented in this collection), has described his own roots as a writer in the oral tale – in his case his own storytelling when a boy:

In one way it began when I was a kid, when I was 'our kiddar', the eldest of a growing family. Before we went to sleep we would tell each other stories, and very quickly I was elected storyteller-in-chief, not only because I was the eldest but because somehow or other it seemed I'd been born with the knack. Like the serials we saw at the pictures (and still see, sometimes, on television) the stories were episodic; but unlike the Harry Carey or Tom Mix serials they didn't end on an exciting note with the hero suspended over the cliff-edge on a taut rope: final cut of the villain brandishing a knife; but drowsily – yawns interrupting, tempo declining, until we were all asleep. We only told each other stories in the dark nights, and especially in the winter when the wind whistled through the window panes and down the chimney, and when the beat of the rain made the perfect background music; in the summer we could read. We were great readers, and the stories we got from books lit up the stories that happened everywhere in real life around us. . . .

Quite early in my career as storyteller, I was supplied with a mundane motive. When my father was on nightshift my mother would whisper to me: 'Try and get them to sleep soon, then get quietly out of bed, and you can slip over to the fish shop for our supper.' On such occasions as this my powers of invention would suffer a sudden decline and my two brothers would be fobbed off with a short – a very short – story. Downstairs my mother would hear the rise and fall of the storyteller's voice come to a finish, and a little later I would creep downstairs with stockings in one hand and trousers in the other: those days we slept in our shirts.

So the ancient oral tradition is still with us, and helps shape the modern short story. However, the short story as we know it today is a relatively modern literary form. You could perhaps look back and see 'short stories' in the Old Testament story of Ruth, or the individual sections of Chaucer's *The Canterbury Tales* (begun in about 1387), or the characters invented by the eighteenth-century periodical writers – such as Ned Drugget, created by Dr Johnson in *The Idler* (1758–60). It is interesting to see how like the modern short story are the tales in verse by George Grabbe (1754–1832). In his most famous, 'Peter Grimes', we read of a cruel fisherman who ill treats his apprentices, and the psychological study of the fisherman and his wretched boy might have come from a modern short story, had it not been in verse:

Pinn'd, beaten, cold, pinch'd, threaten'd and abused –
His efforts punish'd and his food refused, –
Awake tormented, – soon aroused from sleep, –
Struck if he wept, and yet compelled to weep,
The trembling boy dropp'd down and strove to pray,
Received a blow, and trembling turn'd away,
Or sobb'd and hid his piteous face; – while he,

The savage master, grinn'd in horrid glee:
He'd now the power he ever loved to show,
A feeling being subject to his blow.

In England a few prose short stories were written during the nineteenth century, and some consider Sir Walter Scott's 'The Two Drovers', written in 1827, as 'the first modern short story'. However, despite all its interesting precursors, the short story was not established easily. In England the immense popularity of the three-volume novel dominated fiction. Publishers had special arrangements with commercial circulating libraries, and magazines serialized the novels. There was little encouragement for authors to try shorter lengths. Of course, the novel has 'story' in common with 'the short story', but the lengthy form of the novel is essentially different: sub-plots are possible, and variety and contrast are effective, indeed necessary. It was almost as if in England the short story had to wait for the decline of the all-powerful novel.

Later in the nineteenth century the short story, as we know it, was developed in different countries – by the American Edgar Allan Poe (1809–49),the Frenchman Guy de Maupassant (1850–93),the Russian Anton Chekhov (1860–1904), and the American Kate Chopin (1851–1904), whose work until recently has been almost entirely left out of literary histories, largely because of the shocked reaction to her novel *The Awakening*. Those four authors established the short-story form as related to, but different from, the novel; no mere cut-down version. They developed a self-conscious literary awareness of what they were doing, and this can be seen in Poe's definition of a short story, which he wrote in a book review in 1842:

The ordinary novel is objectionable, from its length . . . As it cannot be read at one sitting, it deprives itself, of course, of the immense force derivable from totality. Worldly interests intervening during the pauses of perusal, modify, annul or counteract, to a greater or lesser degree, the impression of the book. But simple cessation in reading would, of itself, be sufficient to destroy the true unity. In the brief tale, however, the author is enabled to carry out the fullness of his intention, be it what it may. During the hour of its perusal the soul of the reader is at the writer's control. There are no external or extrinsic influences – resulting from weariness or interruption.

A skilful literary artist has constructed a tale. If wise, he has not fashioned his thoughts to accommodate his incidents; but having conceived, with deliberate care, a certain unique or single effect to be wrought out, he then invents such incidents – he then combines such effects as may best aid him in establishing this preconceived effect. If his very initial sentence tends not to the outbringing of this effect, then he has failed in his first step. In the whole composition there should be no word written, of which the tendency, direct or indirect, is not to the pre-established design. And by such means, with such care and skill, a picture is at length painted which leaves in the mind of him who contemplates it with a kindred care, a sense of the fullest satisfaction. The idea of the tale has been presented unblemished, because undisturbed; and this is an end unattainable by the novel.

Throughout this century all major writers have devoted some of their energies to the form, and writers such as D. H. Lawrence, James Joyce and E. M. Forster are thought by some critics to be at their best in the form. Other writers such as Katherine Mansfield and V. S. Pritchett have made the short story their main form of writing.

There are two particular traditions of the English short story that are especially interesting: one is the great Irish output and the other is that of the West Indies. It is difficult to explain why the short story has flourished so in Ireland, but it is certainly a form of literature at which the Irish writers had traditionally excelled – and continue to do so. After James Joyce there were Liam O'Flaherty, Frank O'Connor, Sean O'Faolain and Mary Lavin. It is possible that the tradition was established partly because one of the strengths of many of these writers was their closeness to the texture of peasant life, and that the striking picture of a simple moment in rural life is better captured in the short story than the novel.

If Irish short-story writing had its roots in the past, the West Indies virtually created a new literature in the years after about 1950. There was a powerful surge of new writing, stimulated it appeared by the new political self-consciousness and liberation. Writers could draw strength from the tradition of English literature that had been taught in schools and colleges, but they wanted to create their own literature and write about their own lives. The short story was a form that could especially well cope with the range of concerns and at the same time was comparatively easy to publish. The literary magazine *Bim* became more than a mere publishing device; it was almost a school for the emerging writers. Many of the writers studied abroad, and their worldwide perspective when directed at the life of the villages and towns in which they had grown up in the islands gave a depth and tension. Sometimes, as in Naipaul's stories, this could be mocking, and at other times it was tragic. Many of the writers became exiles, and some like Samuel Selvon wrote of their exile. The range of their writing has extended, and there is no such thing as a 'typical' West Indian story. Nevertheless, the body of stories (and, of course, novels) contributed by West Indian writers is an impressive part of today's literature.

This collection

Any anthology must explain why it is as it is, and does not include other examples. As I have already made clear, the riches of the contemporary short story are so great that the problem is deciding how to keep stories out. A number of collections of important and fascinating stories could be made from the writings of the last twenty five years. What, then, are the principles of this volume?

Firstly, all the authors represented here are major authors, writers whose work has not only pleased many interested readers but also been critically recognized. Indeed, the number of major literary awards collected by the authors in this anthology is great.

Secondly, I have chosen writers whose other work, or at least a substantial part of it, could be read with interest and profit by the student reader. Thus, the story by Nadine Gordimer could lead to reading her novel *July's People*, that by V. S. Naipaul to *Miguel Street* or *A Bend in the River*. Susan Hill's story in this collection could lead to reading her fine novels *In the Springtime of the Year*, *I'm the King of the Castle*, or *Strange Meeting* – all powerful and difficult books, but ones enjoyed by student readers. And this is true of each of the other authors.

Thirdly, I have made sure that even though the writers are in most cases known also for their novels, each of them has published substantial collections of short stories, has devoted a considerable part of his or her writing energies to short stories, and is respected especially as a short-story writer. Perhaps only Mary Lavin and V. S. Pritchett are regarded only as writers of short stories, but all of the others owe a major part of their critical esteem to their stories.

Because the collection is designed for students of English literature, all the writers not only write in English, but come from countries thought of as sharing something of the English cultural heritage. There are, therefore, no American authors, nor translations from West Indian or African writers who originally wrote in languages other than English. I have also had in mind the tradition of English literature, and see the stories in this book as the natural successors to key stories by earlier major writers of English literature.

'Today' is a difficult lable. Each of the authors is alive; each still writing; each is regarded as important and worth reading as a contemporary writer. On the other hand, these are all writers who have made their reputations and are very well-established. Indeed they have mostly held their own for many years, and are by no means amongst those who are only just beginning to make a name for themselves. I see them as summing up in their various ways the achievements of the last twenty five years. Of course, other important short-story writers have not been included: I should have liked to have included, for instance, John Wain, Liam O'Flaherty, Gillian Tindall, Fay Weldon, Sean O'Faolain, Ruth Prawer Jhabvala, Muriel Spark, Elizabeth Taylor, Michael Anthony, Frank Sargeson, George Lamming, Edgar Mittelhölzer, Shiva Naipaul, John Hearne, Samuel Selvon and Andrew Salkey (many of them, interestingly, Irish or West Indian). But one volume can only be so long! All these writers are listed in the suggestions for further reading, and I hope that students will sample at least some of them.

The themes of only ten stories cannot hope to cover a whole cross-section of the themes of modern literature, but I have consciously endeavoured to represent many of the major themes of today. Although each of the stories is focused on individual people, and none of them can be crudely labelled as 'political', many of the characters and themes are gripped by outer social or political forces. Nadine Gordimer once said: 'I write about their private selves; often, even in their most private situations, they are what they are because their lives are regulated and their mores (social customs and moral priciples) formed by the political situation.'[4] This is as true of Major Carruthers in 'The Second Hut' as it is of the lovers in 'Country Lovers'; it is also true of Matty in 'The Patriot Son', and even of Martin in 'A Time to Keep' and Lionel in 'The Boss'.

In many cases there are racial tensions behind the stories, surely one of the major concerns of our age. In others, the theme relates to the tension between generations.

In all of them, though, it is human concern that is paramount. The most striking thing about the writers is their ability to evoke what it is like to be human in certain specific circumstances, and through that precision to help us relish the humanity of people more generally. One of the longest stories in the collection is Susan Hill's 'The Custodian', which is a study of the unexpected tenderness and love of an old man for a young boy. Through that description we learn of the love of many people, their generosity, and their sensitivity.

Finally, I have tried to choose stories which are simply very good pieces of literature in their own right, stories that can be read carefully, re-read, pondered and returned to. Each of these is a minor masterpiece.

[1]Pritchett, V. S., Preface to *Collected Stories*, Chatto and Windus, 1982, p xi

[2]Allen, Walter, *The Short Story in English*, Clarendon Press.

[3]Pritchett, V. S., Preface to *Collected Stories*, Chatto and Windus, 1982, pp x and xi

[4]From an interview published in the London Magazine in 1965.

Short Stories for Today

The Patriot Son

Mary Lavin

IT WAS A couple of years since Sean Mongon had set foot in Conerty's shop, so what did he want now?

From the window in the gable-end Matty saw him swinging down the street, and the next minute he walked in the doorway and up to the counter.

'Will you display this in your window, Matty, like a good chap?' he said casually, and he unrolled a cheaply-printed poster, the paper like a blotter, on which lettering had made a blurred impress.

As far as Matty could see it was a play-bill, with a crude picture of a woman in green in the middle of it, and the wording seemed to be in Gaelic, or in Gaelic letters. He partly guessed what it was, and he glanced uneasily across the shop to the haberdashery, where his mother was serving a customer. She never liked any of the Mongons. And although Matty could remember a time when their own shop was just as small as Mongon's, before the new barracks was built opposite them, yet his mother always referred to the Mongons' shop as poky and smelly, and she wondered how people could eat anything that came out of it.

But the Mongons did a good trade; particularly with the farmers from outside the town. Once when he was a child he had asked his mother why the country people did not tie up their traps and donkey-carts in their yard, like they did in Mongon's.

'Because we live opposite the barracks,' she said promptly, and pulling out the till from under the counter she ran the silver through her fingers like water. 'One R.I.C. man coming into the shop with his shilling in his hand is better than twenty traps tied in the yard and the ledgers swelling with debt! God bless the Constabulary!' she said.

And when, at that moment, through the window, they saw the Head Constable walking down the street, with his stomach out and his arms swinging, she shook her head.

'Isn't it a terrible thing to think a fine man like that would have enemies?' she cried.

For a minute he didn't know what she meant.

'Some people never can let bygones be bygones,' she went on. 'It's the Fenian bitterness. It's like a disease that's passed down from father to son. God protect us all!'

He knew then that she was having a dig at the Mongons, because Sean's grandfather had been a Fenian. The Mongons had his uniform in a box on top of the piano. Sean brought him in to see it one day after school. But he had been careful not to tell his mother about it. She was death on the Fenians.

'Oh, you know nothing of what people suffered in those days, son!' she said.

They were in the kitchen at the time of this conversation. He was sitting at the kitchen table doing his homework and she was standing stirring a pot on the range. But she was looking out of the window and after a few minutes she gave a big sigh.

'It would be a terrible thing if it were all to break out again,' she said softly, almost to herself, and the look on her face frightened the wits out of him.

'What do you mean, Mother?' he cried.

She turned to him.

'I'm afraid, son, there is some of the bad old seed still in the ground,' she said. 'The Head Constable was in the shop a while ago and he told me something: there are men drilling in the hills again!' She looked away for a minute, and then she turned and looked steadily at his face. 'Thank God you're only a child still,' she said.

Matty squirmed uncomfortably on his chair; he wasn't such a child at all: the following year he'd be leaving school.

It was just before the end of that year that the Gaelic classes were started. They were to be held at night in the school-house, and Master Cullen was giving his services free as teacher. Needless to say, Sean Mongon was the first to join them.

'Oh, come on, Matty,' he cried. 'Join up! We'll have great sport at them. And afterwards, to warm us up, the Master says he'll push back the benches and have a bit of a dance. It'll be great sport. The Master knows all the old jigs and reels, and the Walls of Limerick, and the Bridge of Athlone. We'll have the best of times!'

For his own part, Matty was inclined to go to the classes, just to be in the swim of things. But he was uneasy about what his mother would say. He knew her views on the Language Revival.

'What next?' she demanded, when she first read about the Gaelic League, and the language classes that were being held in Dublin. 'Do they want to drive the people backward instead of forward?'

He'd never have the face to tell her he was going to the classes.

'I'll have to ask my mother,' he said, shamefacedly.

Sean looked at him, at first incredulous, then contemptuous.

'Maybe you ought to ask leave of the R.I.C. as well!' he said. 'It wouldn't do to offend them, they're such good customers!'

Matty felt his face flush all over. And Sean saw it.

'Sorry!' he said, surprisingly, and his smile, that was always so winning, flashed across his face. 'I'm a bit on edge these days,' he said. 'No hard feelings, eh? It's just that we don't want the R.I.C. poking their noses into the classes. The next thing they'd be branding them as illegal organizations! They're terrible eejits in spite of everything.'

Did he fancy it, Matty wondered, or did Sean look at him slyly before he sauntered away. Anyway, he did not go to the classes that winter. And the next winter, although he had left school, he did not go to them either, in spite of the fact that by then the Gaelic League had got itself accepted all over the country, and had established centres in every town and village. As for Master Cullen's classes, they were held openly and boldly. Nearly all the young people in the town went to them, and some of the older people used to go down and stand at the door later in the evenings to look at the dancing. The R.I.C. themselves used to stroll down sometimes and stand in the doorway.

Matty's mother could hardly object to him joining the classes then, but she kept him so late in the shop, and he was so dog-tired when the shutters were put up at last, that by the time he got down to the school-house it wasn't worth while doing anything but hang about the door with the other onlookers. It all seemed very harmless; and he was aware only of the heat and the dust, the sweating faces of the men, the clapping of hands, and the stamping of feet.

But there were other nights when it was too late to go down at all, and then, looking out of the window as he was going to bed, the school-house lights, twinkling across the roofs of the other houses, troubled him, as he used to be troubled when he was a child by tales of faery lights that shone on the darksome bog to lure men to folly and destruction.

It was on those occasions that he was glad his mother had kept him from getting involved in what went on down there. He had begun to wonder if it was all as innocent as it seemed.

And now this play? Was it only what it purported to be; a little entertainment: or was there some undercurrent of intrigue? He looked dubiously at the play-bill he was being asked to display.

But Sean saw his hesitation, and he laughed.

'There are no flies on you, Matty, are there?' he said, and he winked, but affably, and not with any pronounced discretion. Suddenly he leant across the counter. 'It's supposed to be *The Colleen Bawn*,' he said, 'but we've doctored a good few of the lines. Do you get me? It's going a bit further than Irish classes, and jigs and reels, but it's time we showed more guts. Things have changed, haven't they?' he said, and he laughed, and jerked his head in the direction of the barracks across the street. 'We've moved forward since the time we were nervous about the classes at night in the school-house! They know all about them now; or at least they think they do: but they're afraid to take any action in case they might mistake the sheep for the goats. They don't know who to trust, and who to mistrust. And that's the way to have them. I hear they're even beginning to distrust each other. And so well they might. Did you see in the papers where an R.I.C. man down in –'

5

But at this moment, across the shop Matty caught his mother's baleful eye upon him, and he saw that outside the counter there was a small child with a halfpenny in its hand.

'Excuse me a minute, Sean,' he said awkwardly. 'I'll have to wait on this youngster.'

He hoped he'd go. But instead, Mongon took up the play-bill.

'I'll put this in the window for you. I think that's the best place for it, don't you?' he said, leaning into the window and draping it across the job lot of cups and saucers that were being offered that week at a special price.

When the youngster had gone he turned back to Matty.

'Do you know what I was thinking?' he said, and he chuckled. 'I was thinking that it's a picture of you we ought to have on the poster – a bloody little shopkeeper – and a banner around your arm to say that you were the Ireland of Today!'

Matty stared at him. Was he trying to be funny, he wondered. If so, it was a poor joke, specially when his mother could probably overhear everything that was said.

But Sean didn't seem to be joking, or at least he didn't look very light-hearted.

'Poor ignorant Ireland,' he said suddenly, in a low voice, as if to himself. 'Poor ignorant Ireland that doesn't want to be saved!'

Matty shrugged his shoulders. He must be cracked, he decided. And he wished harder than ever he would go about his business.

But still Sean stayed, leaning against the counter and looking around him.

'It's a long time since I was here, isn't it?' he said. 'But it's the same old place I see. You haven't made any changes, have you?' His eye strayed idly, it would seem, all over the shop and came to rest on the green baize door at the end. 'That door leads into the house, doesn't it?' he asked, pointing to it. 'Isn't that the way we used to run in and out the yard?'

'I suppose so,' said Matty flatly. He wanted to get rid of him.

He could feel his mother's eyes boring holes in his head.

At long last Sean went.

'Well, so long!' he said inconsequentially, and sauntered out.

Partly drawn by the old fascination that the other always exerted on him, and partly to avoid meeting his mother's eyes, Matty went over to the gable window and looked up the street after him, but he could hear his mother crossing the shop and almost immediately she came and stood beside him looking out of the window.

'You ought to be more careful about who you're seen talking to nowadays, Matty,' she said, lowering her voice although they were alone. 'The Sergeant was telling me that several people in this town are under observation. I shouldn't be surprised if Sean Mongon was one of them. I hope he won't make a habit of coming down here. What did he want, anyway?'

Before he had time to tell her, however, she had seen the play-bill draped across the things in the window. Instantly she whipped it out of the window.

'So this is what brought him down here, is it?' she cried, and as she read it her eyes blazed. The next minute she tore it savagely in two bits. Matty was sure she was going to turn on him, but instead she spoke surprisingly gently, almost wheedlingly to him. 'I suppose you were right to let on we'd display it,' she said, 'but wouldn't it be an awful thing if you forgot to take it out of the window and the Head Constable passed and saw it?'

Matty looked at the torn poster. She had made it seem as if he would have torn it up if she hadn't done so.

It might be uncomfortable all right, he thought, to have had it in the window if the Head Constable came into the shop. But it would be ten times more uncomfortable if Sean came back and did not see it displayed anywhere.

What would he do then, he thought miserably? He wished she wouldn't interfere with everything he did. She was an interfering woman if ever there was one. Ever since he was a child. She had dictated to him in everything. Always the same, he thought bitterly. He'd never get a chance to say or do anything while she had her foot on his neck. And he'd never get away from her, because she'd never let him look at a girl, much less marry one, and bring her into the house. There wasn't a girl in the whole town that would have the courage to marry him, and come into the same house as her.

And then, freakishly, there flashed into his mind the image of the girl on the play-bill, and although he had only barely glimpsed her, it seemed as if she had some enormous strength or power that would vanquish any enemy – even his mother.

A paper woman! I must be cracked, he thought, and he set his mind to think of some excuse to make to Sean if he happened to find out they hadn't displayed the poster.

But it was to be three or four weeks before he met Sean again. And the circumstances of the meeting put the poster out of their minds.

One evening Matty had finished up earlier than usual and he had taken it into his head to stroll down to the school-house to watch the dancing. But when he turned into the school-yard to his surprise the school-house windows were dark and the building was empty. He went up to the door and rattled the handle. The door was locked. As he raised his head though, on the sweet spring air he got the faint smell of cigarette smoke, and looking down he saw that the gravel under his feet was marked with fresh footprints and the tyre-marks of bicycles. So they had been here! But why had they gone so early?

Uneasily he moved away from the black shadow of the building into the open moonlit yard. A ridiculous notion passed through his mind: the faery light! Had it lured them away – the gay throng – away from their warm habitations to the cold inhuman hills and the dark glensides?

A shiver ran over him, but he laughed at himself for his foolishness, and he went home to bed.

But he slept badly, disturbed by dreams of faery hosts and lonely glens, and woke when the dawn was coming up the sky. He got to his feet and went to the window.

There was nothing to be seen but the sight that had met his eyes every day since he was born, the ugly concrete walls of the new barracks, and the corrugated roofs of its sheds and out-houses.

Then, just as he was about to get back into bed, between the barracks and the corrugated sheds, he caught a glimpse of the green, dawn-lit fields beyond the town. And as they had never done in full daylight, those green fields called to him: a clear, sweet call. Unquestioningly he answered their call and in a few minutes he was stealing down the stairs so as not to waken his mother. In the street he paused too, and glanced uneasily at the windows of the barracks. The Constabulary, if they happened to see him, might think it odd of him to be out so early. For the rumours of men drilling were no longer so vague. All over the country men were drilling. And people who were not involved were careful to avoid doing anything irregular. But there was no one on foot in the barracks, and he passed unnoticed out of the town.

About two miles outside the town there was an old deserted castle sunk deep in the middle of a lush, waterlogged field. Sometimes in summer he used to cross the field and wander in its dark passages and vaulted arcades, but in winter it was a lonely place, and only served him as a landmark. At this point he usually turned homeward. This morning too, he was about to turn upon coming in sight of it, when his eye was caught by a thin feather of smoke wavering in the air from one of the thick buttressed chimneys. And almost at the same moment, on the other side of the hedge beside the road, he heard a sound of splashing in the little stream that had for some distance run along beneath the hedge.

Impulsively he called out and bent over the hedge.

To his astonishment it was Sean Mongon. For a minute it looked as if he was going to turn tail and run, until he saw it was Matty.

'Oh, it's only you!' he cried.

But Matty was stung to the quick by his tone.

'Who did you think it was?' he cried, nettled. 'Did you think it was the Constabulary?'

Still, he didn't expect Sean to take him up so sharply.

'How much do you know, Conerty?' he said.

Matty stared. There he was – Sean Mongon – whom he had known all his life; there he was – on the other side of the hedge too – a puny figure really, as slight as a girl, and looking – he noted – haggard and worn-out as if for want of sleep, and yet he was in some way a menacing, a dangerous figure.

But it was not fear that surged up in Matty, it was a grudging admiration.

'I don't know anything,' he said truthfully, even sadly. 'I wish I did!' he added with such fervour that Sean stared at him. 'Yes,' he cried recklessly, 'I wish I was in it – whatever it is, that is going on – I always did, but my mother came between me and it – the Movement, I mean,' he said out boldly.

Sean continued to stare at him.

'I wonder do you mean that,' he said soberly. 'I think you do. And I'm glad to hear you say it – at least. But it's too late now, Matty. You'll have to continue to be one of the onlookers.' He was making a reference to the Gaelic classes, thought Matty, and he felt ashamed of how early his caution had taken command of him. 'Go back to your shop, Matty,' said Sean then, gently, but with a tone of authority. 'The shopboys will soon be taking down the shutters and your mother will be wondering why you're not up and about your business. She'll be knocking at your door. Get back as fast as you can. You don't want her asking questions, do you? That wouldn't help us, you know!' He himself glanced to the east where the rapidly rising sun was striking through the trees as through a grille. 'I must be getting along,' he said in his casual way, and he began to stride back in the direction of the old castle, leaving Matty to stare disconsolately after him.

He was in his bare feet, Matty noticed, with his trousers rolled up, and the wet grass had stuck to his ankles, striping his white skin.

It was something that he had been trusted to keep silent, he thought bitterly, as he walked homeward in dejection.

In the town the shutters were still up on the shop-windows, and when he reached his own street he saw that even the barrack door was shut, and there was no smoke from its chimneys. Except for an old man pushing a handcart of straw in front of him, there was no sign of life in the whole street. And even the old man had a grotesque aspect, like a figure out of a dream, with his ragged clothes and his ramshackle handcart, one wheel of which was wobbling about as if at any moment it would roll from under the cart and let it down on the cobbles.

Amused, Matty followed the wobbly movement of the old man and his cart, and then, just as he was about to turn in to his own door, the wheel, with one last wobble, fell flat on the street, and the cart came down on its axle with a clatter, up-ending its load.

As the old fellow let out a loud volley of oaths, Matty laughed heartily. And from the barrack door which opened, one of the constables poked out his head and laughed also, and nodded across at Matty. There seemed no more to the incident, and Matty went into the shop to begin his day's work. Later in the morning, as he was lending a hand in taking down the shutters, he saw the old fellow trying to raise the wheel, but when he put his hand on it, the rotted wood came away from the rim and the whole thing fell flat again. So, after some words with the police, the old fellow shrugged his shoulders and went off up the street, presumably to find some means of putting his vehicle into motion again, or of getting some other conveyance to cart away the straw that, in the crisp breezes of the morning, was beginning to blow about the street. Already it had almost blocked up the mouth of the barracks.

But the police, as they came in and out of the shop during the day for their cigarettes and tobacco, took it in good part. It was his own mother who took it badly.

'A nice thing!' she cried, a score of times, or more, as she went to the window and looked out. 'A nice mess!'

It was when she was looking out on one of these occasions, late in the day, that Matty saw her frown, and looking over her shoulder he saw Sean coming down the street.

'What does this fellow want now?' she cried, and as if unable to endure the sight of him, she left the shop.

As for Matty, the incident of the upset cart in the street had taken his mind off the events of the earlier morning, but now, at the sight of Sean, his heart began to beat violently.

Had Sean come to look for him? He hurried forward to meet him. But Sean was calm and matter-of-fact.

'Hello, Matty,' he said easily, naturally. 'Can you spare me a few cans of paraffin oil?'

It was a bit of an anti-climax, and it made Matty cranky. He had only come on business. Ostentatiously, Sean threw down a pound note on the counter.

For a minute Matty hesitated. There was only a small profit on paraffin oil, and it was a troublesome commodity; it had to be kept outside the shop in the lobby near the yard door, and anyone handling it had to be careful not to contaminate anything else with the smell of it, and so it was usual only to supply it to regular customers.

'I'm sorry to bother you,' said Sean, as if he sensed Matty's reluctance. 'I'm not a customer, I know.' He paused. 'We usually get it in Flynn's, but – well, they didn't have any today,' he finished lamely.

'Oh, that's all right,' said Matty, and he began to take off his shop-coat. 'Have you got a can?' he asked, unable to resist making a compliment of giving it, but he regretted it next minute, as Sean began to make excuses. 'Oh, it doesn't matter, it's all right,' he said hastily. 'This way!' And he went out through the baize door into the little lobby where the big storage tank was kept. There he stooped down, and picked up a can. 'How much will I give you?' he asked.

But Sean was hardly heeding him as he stared around the lobby.

'Oh, fill it up,' he said casually, and going over to the door leading into the yard, he opened it and looked out. 'It's the same old place,' he said. 'I remember it well. I could make my way around here blindfold!' He stepped back and pointed to the other door, the house door, as it was called, that was opposite the baize door. 'That's the way into the front of the house, isn't it?' he asked. 'We used to go out into the street that way.'

But like the last time he heard them, these reminiscences of their boyish friendship sounded empty to Matty. He ignored them.

'It holds a gallon,' he said, putting a cap on the tin, and holding it out to him.

But Sean was peering into a dark corner behind the tank and the wall, and seeing a few old cans thrown together in a heap, he took up two with one hand and three with the other.

'Fill these up too, will you?' he said casually.

Matty was both irritated and surprised.

'Have you a car?' he asked, as he filled the fourth can.

'No,' said Sean shortly, 'but I'll manage them all right.' He took up two of the cans. 'I'll take these with me, and I'll call back for the rest. You can leave them somewhere convenient to the street. Better still, I'll leave them all and I'll get some kind of conveyance for them. But it may be late in the evening; the shop will probably be closed: you'd better leave them in the front hall, if you can manage it. Just inside the hall door would be the best place,' he said. Then he straightened up. 'Have you got that?' he said, in what Matty thought an impudent manner for one who was under a compliment to him. But evidently there was no offence meant, because Sean stooped and lifted two of the cans. 'I'll give you a hand,' he said. 'We may as well leave them out there now so there'll be no mistake.'

'Oh, there's no need,' said Matty.

He was wondering what his mother would say to cluttering up the front hall, but he decided that she seldom went into the hall anyway, and that it was so dark and dingy she might not see them even if she did go into it. He would prefer to put them there himself a little later. 'That'll be all right,' he repeated as he put the lid on the big drum of oil. Without waiting for him, Sean was about to go away, but on an impulse he turned around.

'Is there much left in the drum?' he asked.

Thinking he wanted more, Matty slapped the lid down ostentatiously.

'A few gallons,' he said, 'but I can't give you any more. I can't empty the tank for you. It wouldn't do to let our regular customers go short.'

'Oh, I don't want any more,' said Sean. 'I have more than enough. I just thought it might be no harm if that drum was empty tonight.'

Matty looked up. It was the kind of cryptic remark that lately he seemed to be hearing on all sides, and he was inclined to let it pass, but all at once a thought flashed into his mind – but it was too preposterous.

'You're not – you can't mean –?'

And then he remembered the cart-load of straw that still, at that late hour, stood outside the barracks. And without another word being spoken he knew all.

'You can't do it!' he cried. 'You'd be mad to try it!'

'Don't shout, you fool!' snapped Sean. Then, with less urgency, and speaking in a lower voice, he looked at Matty with something approximating to admiration. 'I didn't think you were so quick on the uptake,' he said, but he had moved nearer, and feeling him uncomfortably close in the small lobby, Matty looked down and saw that from his pocket there protruded the point of a gun. 'I only meant to do you a good turn, Matty,' said Sean, 'but take care you don't turn good into bad.'

Matty swallowed hard.

'I don't know what you mean!'

Immediately Sean stepped back from him.

'That's the right attitude to take!' he cried, slapping his thigh. 'I told you nothing. And you guessed nothing. See!'

Matty kept steady, although he was appalled.

'All right, Sean. You can trust me.'

Visibly, for a moment, the other relaxed.

'I know that,' he said. Then he got tense again. 'It's not only my own trust I'm putting in you,' he said savagely, 'but the trust of twenty or thirty men – perhaps even the trust of the whole Movement –'

Although he had begun to shudder violently, Matty's eyes did not falter.

'I know that,' he said steadily.

'I think you do,' said Sean soberly. Then suddenly he gave a kick to the cans. 'I won't wait to leave them out in the hall,' he said. 'You can do it for me.'

It was only an errand fit for a child, but it carried the implication of an enormous trust. Speechless, Matty nodded his head. His face was deadly white, and seeing that, perhaps, Sean put out a hand and rested it upon his shoulder.

'Look here,' he said, 'I told you nothing – we've agreed upon that – but there's no reason why you shouldn't empty that thing down the drain' – he nodded at the drum – 'and as a matter of fact, you might find some reason for being away from here tonight. Not that I think there'll be any danger, but I admit the street is narrow and a lot depends on the way the wind is blowing – you'd never know – you could take anything valuable with you – money or the like – nothing that would be remarkable, of course – nothing that would attract attention.'

The suggestion was meant to be friendly, Matty knew that. But at the same time he felt there was something belittling in the concession.

'Thanks, Sean,' he said quietly, 'but I think I'll stay here.' Then, with dismay, he remembered his mother. 'Oh, what about my mother?' he cried. 'I suppose she ought to be got out of here?'

Sean only shrugged his shoulders.

'If you can manage it without it appearing odd,' he said, 'to her, I mean.'

'You can leave it to me,' said Matty, wanting to reassure him. 'I won't make a false step.'

Like sunlight in the dingy lobby, Sean's smile broke over him.
'He that is not against me is with me, eh?' he said, and
turning back towards the shop, he went out that way.

Picking up the cans in twos, Matty carried them into the hall.

It was dark there all right, and getting darker too, because
already the day had begun to fade. With a little feeling of relief
he realized that at least there would not be long hours of
suspense. Whatever was to happen would be likely to commence
soon enough. It was not yet time for the shop to close, but the
shutters had already been brought in from the yard and stood
against the wall. Once the shop was closed he need not worry
if his mother found the tins. It would appear fairly reasonable
then that they were left convenient to the hall door.

The shop was over an hour closed when she discovered them.

'Matty, what is all this paraffin doing here?' she cried.

Matty was at the back of the house, afraid that he might give
anything away by looking out too often if he were in any of the
front rooms. But just as he wondered what answer to give to
her, with every nerve thrilling, his strained ears caught a sound
in the street. Ignoring all but that sound, he stood transfixed.

His mother too heard something.

'Was that a shout?' she said, coming back from the hall, her
face white. 'Listen!' she commanded. 'The Constabulary are
challenging someone!'

But there was another sound, fainter than shout or challenge,
which caught Matty's ear. It was a faint crackling sound, and
the next minute he smelled something smouldering. Then his
mother too got the smell.

'Oh, good God!' she cried. 'It's a fire – it's the barracks. The
barracks is burning!' She made as if to rush out to the street,
but he put out his arm. She strained to pass him. 'Will you let
me pass?' she cried. 'What's the matter with you?'

It was something in the expression on his face that answered
her.

'Oh, God!' she whispered, no longer straining against him.
'It's not malicious, is it?'

Malicious! It was a word out of the civilian life from which, without knowing it until that moment, he had already long since passed. Malicious: more than all the words that one by one had measured the difference between them since he was a child, this one word showed them to be sundered for ever. But he said nothing. Feverishly she was making the Sign of the Cross.

'Oh, God help them!' she whispered. 'Caught like rats in a trap.' Then, suddenly, her thoughts veered. 'Which way is the wind?' she cried. 'Are the sparks flying this way?' She swung around towards the lobby. 'The oil drum,' she exclaimed. 'One spark would be enough –'

But before one thought was completed, another had taken its place.

'Those cans in the hall,' she cried. 'Get them out of there.' And when he didn't move, she darted towards the door. He caught her by the arm.

'Leave them there, Mother,' he said. 'They may be coming for them any minute.'

They? She turned around. And then the full enormity of the truth broke over her.

'Oh, God in Heaven!' she cried. 'It wasn't for that you sold the oil? You don't mean to say you knew all about it and you never told me – we could have warned them – we could have –' She wrung her hands. 'We could have done something,' she groaned. Then all at once she pulled herself together. 'Perhaps it's not too late yet. Those cans in the hall, you say they're coming back for them! I'll spoil their game there, anyway. Never mind about what's done: it can't be helped. Please God they'll never find out you had any hand in it –' She had broken away from him and reached the door, but at the door she couldn't help turning around. 'Oh, how could you do it?' she cried. 'Haven't I been all my life warning you against the like? Do you think a handful of fools are going to get the better of trained men like the R.I.C.? The constabulary will make bits of them, I tell you. And you along with them if they find out about these – but with God's help they won't find out. Here, give me a hand!'

As she caught up the cans, however, the voices in the street became louder, and there was a sound of running feet followed by a crash against the door behind which they stood, and then heavily, frantically, two fists beat against the panels.

'It's Sean! He wants the cans,' said Matty, 'and he's going to get them too,' he cried, as he tried to drag the cans out of her hand.

But the fists beat against the door again.

'Let me in, for Christ's sake,' said a voice. It was Sean all right. 'Don't mind the bloody cans but open the door.'

Both together, mother and son, let go the cans, and the oil spilled over the floor. In a second the hall was filled with the acrid smell. But they had both let go from different motives.

'Don't dare to open that door!' screamed the woman, and she threw herself forward.

But Matty had got there before her and the door was open.

Almost falling over them, Sean lurched forward.

'Why the hell didn't you open the door?' he rasped, as he stood panting and trying to get his breath. 'Close it now, you fool,' he cried, as hypnotized, Matty stood looking at him. 'Close it and lock it,' he cried. 'Put on those chains,' he cried, pointing to the rusty old chain that hung down inside it but was never used. 'The whole thing failed,' he said when he got his breath.

Matty looked up.

'I didn't –' he began.

'I know that,' said Sean, and he gave a bitter laugh. 'You'd be a dead bunny now if you did! No, it was the bloody straw let us down – it got damp, I suppose, out there in the street all evening; it wouldn't catch when we went to set fire to it – it only smouldered, and the beggars smelled the smoke. But we got away,' he cried. 'That's one good thing. And if we failed tonight, we won't fail the next time. Listen!' he said. 'They're searching the street, but I don't suppose they'll think of trying here.' He gave the dry laugh again. 'They'd never suspect you of being a patriot!' he said.

But there were sounds of someone approaching.

'What's that?' cried Sean, alert again.

'They're coming over here,' whispered Matty, the sweat pouring from him. 'Listen!'

Sean listened.

'I was expecting too much,' he said calmly. 'I'll have to get moving,' and he ran into the back lobby. But as he passed the oil vat he stopped. 'I'll throw this thing in here in the dark,' he said, and dragging off the old whitish trench-coat that was like a second skin to him, it was constantly on his back, he threw it behind the oil drum. 'I'll travel lighter without it,' he cried, 'and besides, it's too easily seen at night.'

They had forgotten the old woman, but as, at that moment, there was a violent knocking on the door, they became aware of her again. She was dragging at the chain and bolts.

'It's all right, constable,' she was shouting. 'I'm opening it as quick as I can. He's gone out the back way!'

Like a flame from the abortive fire, Matty felt shame run over him. But even in that preposterous moment, Sean put out a hand and laid it for an instant on his shoulder.

'It isn't your fault,' he said, and then as the yard door opened before him he prepared to plunge into the darkness. But on the brink he hesitated, and suddenly he turned back. 'Wait a minute! She may have done me more good than harm,' he cried. 'Prop open this door, like as if it was usually kept open – with that,' he cried, indicating with his foot an old iron weight on the floor. Then, with a last reckless laugh at Matty's stupefaction, he slipped behind the propped door.

It was so simple. Matty stared stupidly. He hardly understood, but it was a chance, he could see that; even if it was only a small one. As long as his mother hadn't seen them! But the oil drum was behind them, and the view from the front hall was broken by the cross-door that had almost closed after them. It might work out!

A tremendous excitement possessed him. If only there was something he could do! If he could put the police off the scent!

Suddenly, behind the big oil drum, he caught sight of the old trench coat bundled into a ball. He rushed over and pulled it out.

The next minute he heard the front door crash open and the constabulary rushed into the hall.

Pulling the old trench-coat over him, Matty ran to the yard door, but on the threshold he waited for an instant till he heard the running feet reach the cross-door. They must catch a glimpse of him. The next minute he was racing across the yard.

What was it Sean planned to do? To get across the sheds and out into the next yard, and from there into the next, and the next?

As kids they used to scramble up on the sheds, but although he made for the lowest of them, the little pig-shed, in the corner, he found he wasn't as agile as he used to be. Still he managed to grasp the ragged edge of the corrugated-iron roof and frantically he began to pull himself up on it. As his head came level with the tin he saw that although the yard was dark, it was dark from being overhung with buildings; above him the sky was brilliant with stars. And all at once, compounded out of the very stars it seemed, a spirit of elation flowed through him, such as he had never before experienced. And it seemed as if something that had eluded him all his life was all at once within his grasp.

Pushing his hands further forward on the rusty iron, and letting go his foothold, he exerted a tremendous pressure and heaved his body upward. But the next moment the house behind him was filled with shouts and then – as loud as if they had rained into his mouth, his eyes, his ears – the air was shattered with shots. And at the same moment he felt a ripping pain run like the jag of a knife down the side of his belly.

They got me, he thought, as he fell forward on his face. But the thought did nothing to dispel his elation which seemed only to grow greater, until in a kind of intoxication of excitement he lay there, feeling the hot blood trickling down inside his torn clothes.

It was a few minutes before it occurred to him that it was odd that they had not come looking for him. From where he lay, by raising his head, he could see the house, and the lighted door through which he had run out. No one had come through it! They were all still inside, the police, and – yes – his mother too. With difficulty he raised his head: they were bending over something. At first it looked like an old sack of potatoes, but as it twitched suddenly he saw it was a body: the body of Sean Mongon.

And at the same moment, the pain that had lacerated him tore again into his guts, and putting down his hand he felt the jagged fang of the rusted iron that had cut into him like a bullet.

Then his mother's voice came clear above the other voices that now were in the yard below him.

'He's up there on the top of the pig-shed!' she cried, and her voice was wheedling. 'He must have been frightened out of his wits!' she said.

And coming nearer, she called up to him:

'Come down out of that, you gom!'

Country Lovers

Nadine Gordimer

THE FARM CHILDREN play together when they are small; but once the white children go away to school they soon don't play together any more, even in the holidays. Although most of the black children get some sort of schooling, they drop every year farther behind the grades passed by the white children; the childish vocabulary, the child's exploration of the adventurous possibilities of dam, koppies, mealie lands and veld – there comes a time when the white children have surpassed these with the vocabulary of boarding-school and the possibilities of inter-school sports matches and the kind of adventures seen at the cinema. This usefully coincides with the age of twelve or thirteen; so that by the time early adolescence is reached, the black children are making, along with the bodily changes common to all, an easy transition to adult forms of address, beginning to call their old playmates *missus* and *baasie* – little master.

The trouble was Paulus Eysendyck did not seem to realize that Thebedi was now simply one of the crowd of farm children down at the kraal, recognizable in his sisters' old clothes. The first Christmas holidays after he had gone to boarding-school he brought home for Thebedi a painted box he had made in his wood-work class. He had to give it to her secretly because he had nothing for the other children at the kraal. And she gave him, before he went back to school, a bracelet she had made of thin brass wire and the grey-and-white beans of the castor-oil crop his father cultivated. (When they used to play together, she was the one who had taught Paulus how to make clay oxen for their toy spans.) There was a craze, even in the *platteland* towns like the one where he was at school, for boys to wear elephant-hair and other bracelets beside their watch-straps; his was admired, friends asked him to get similar ones for them. He said the natives made them on his father's farm and he would try.

When he was fifteen, six feet tall, and tramping round at school dances with the girls from the 'sister' school in the same town; when he had learnt how to tease and flirt and fondle quite intimately these girls who were the daughters of prosperous farmers like his father; when he had even met one who, at a wedding he had attended with his parents on a nearby farm, had let him do with her in a locked storeroom what people did when they made love – when he was as far from his childhood as all this, he still brought home from a shop in town a red plastic belt and gilt hoop ear-rings for the black girl, Thebedi. She told her father the missus had given these to her as a reward for some work she had done – it was true she sometimes was called to help out in the farmhouse. She told the girls in the kraal that she had a sweetheart nobody knew about, far away, away on another farm, and they giggled, and teased, and admired her. There was a boy in the kraal called Njabulo who said he wished he could have bought her a belt and ear-rings.

When the farmer's son was home for the holidays she wandered far from the kraal and her companions. He went for walks alone. They had not arranged this; it was an urge each followed independently. He knew it was she, from a long way off. She knew that his dog would not bark at her. Down at the dried-up river-bed where five or six years ago the children had caught a leguaan one great day – a creature that combined ideally the size and ferocious aspect of the crocodile with the harmlessness of the lizard – they squatted side by side on the earth bank. He told her traveller's tales: about school, about the punishments at school, particularly, exaggerating both their nature and his indifference to them. He told her about the town of Middleburg, which she had never seen. She had nothing to tell but she prompted with many questions, like any good listener. While he talked he twisted and tugged at the roots of white stinkwood and Cape willow trees that looped out of the eroded earth around them. It had always been a good spot for children's games, down there hidden by the mesh of old, ant-eaten trees held in place by vigorous ones, wild asparagus bushing up between the trunks, and here and there prickly-pear cactus sunken-skinned and bristly, like an old man's face, keeping alive sapless until the next rainy season. She punctured the dry hide of a prickly-pear again and again with a sharp stick

while she listened. She laughed a lot at what he told her, sometimes dropping her face on her knees, sharing amusement with
the cool shady earth beneath her bare feet. She put on her pair
of shoes – white sandals, thickly Blanco-ed against the farm dust
– when he was on the farm, but these were taken off and laid
aside, at the river-bed.

One summer afternoon when there was water flowing there
and it was very hot she waded in as they used to do when they
were children, her dress bunched modestly and tucked into the
legs of her pants. The schoolgirls he went swimming with at
dams or pools on neighbouring farms wore bikinis but the sight
of their dazzling bellies and thighs in the sunlight had never
made him feel what he felt now, when the girl came up the bank
and sat beside him, the drops of water beading off her dark legs
the only points of light in the earth-smelling, deep shade. They
were not afraid of one another, they had known one another
always; he did with her what he had done that time in the
storeroom at the wedding, and this time it was so lovely, so
lovely, he was surprised . . . and she was surprised by it, too
– he could see in her dark face that was part of the shade, with
her big dark eyes, shiny as soft water, watching him attentively:
as she had when they used to huddle over their teams of mud
oxen, as she had when he told her about detention weekends
at school.

They went to the river-bed often through those summer
holidays. They met just before the light went, as it does quite
quickly, and each returned home with the dark – she to her
mother's hut, he to the farmhouse – in time for the evening
meal. He did not tell her about school or town any more. She
did not ask questions any longer. He told her, each time, when
they would meet again. Once or twice it was very early in the
morning; the lowing of the cows being driven to graze came to
them where they lay, dividing them with unspoken recognition
of the sound read in their two pairs of eyes, opening so close to
each other.

He was a popular boy at school. He was in the second, then

the first soccer team. The head girl of the 'sister' school was said to have a crush on him; he didn't particularly like her, but there was a pretty blonde who put up her long hair into a kind of doughnut with a black ribbon round it, whom he took to see films when the schoolboys and girls had a free Saturday afternoon. He had been driving tractors and other farm vehicles since he was ten years old, and as soon as he was eighteen he got a driver's licence and in the holidays, this last year of his school-life, he took neighbours' daughters to dances and to the drive-in cinema that had just opened twenty kilometres from the farm. His sisters were married, by then; his parents often left him in charge of the farm over the weekend while they visited the young wives and grandchildren.

When Thebedi saw the farmer and his wife drive away on a Saturday afternoon, the boot of their Mercedes filled with fresh-killed poultry and vegetables from the garden that it was part of her father's work to tend, she knew that she must come not to the river-bed but up to the house. The house was an old one, thick-walled, dark against the heat. The kitchen was its lively thoroughfare, with servants, food supplies, begging cats and dogs, pots boiling over, washing being damped for ironing, and the big deep-freeze the missus had ordered from town, bearing a crocheted mat and a vase of plastic irises. But the dining-room with the bulging-legged heavy table was shut up in its rich, old smell of soup and tomato sauce. The sitting-room curtains were drawn and the TV set silent. The door of the parents' bedroom was locked and the empty rooms where the girls had slept had sheets of plastic spread over the beds. It was in one of these that she and the farmer's son stayed together whole nights – almost: she had to get away before the house servants, who knew her, came in at dawn. There was a risk someone would discover her or traces of her presence if he took her to his own bedroom, although she had looked into it many times when she was helping out in the house and knew well, there, the row of silver cups he had won at school.

When she was eighteen and the farmer's son nineteen and

27

working with his father on the farm before entering a veterinary college, the young man Njabulo asked her father for her. Njabulo's parents met with hers and the money he was to pay in place of the cows it is customary to give a prospective bride's parents was settled upon. He had no cows to offer; he was a labourer on the Eysendyck farm, like her father. A bright youngster; old Eysendyck had taught him bricklaying and was using him for odd jobs in construction, around the place. She did not tell the farmer's son that her parents had arranged for her to marry. She did not tell him, either, before he left for his first term at the veterinary college, that she thought she was going to have a baby. Two months after her marriage to Njabulo, she gave birth to a daughter. There was no disgrace in that; among her people it is customary for a young man to make sure, before marriage, that the chosen girl is not barren, and Njabulo had made love to her then. But the infant was very light and did not quickly grow darker as most African babies do. Already at birth there was on its head a quantity of straight, fine floss, like that which carries the seeds of certain weeds in the veld. The unfocused eyes it opened were grey flecked with yellow. Njabulo was the matt, opaque coffee-grounds colour that has always been called black; the colour of Thebedi's legs on which beaded water looked oyster-shell blue, the same colour as Thebedi's face, where the black eyes, with their interested gaze and clear whites, were so dominant.

Njabulo made no complaint. Out of his farm labourer's earnings he bought from the Indian store a cellophane-windowed pack containing a pink plastic bath, six napkins, a card of safety pins, a knitted jacket, cap and bootees, a dress, and a tin of Johnson's Baby Powder, for Thebedi's baby.

When it was two weeks old Paulus Eysendyck arrived home from the veterinary college for the holidays. He drank a glass of fresh, still-warm milk in the childhood familiarity of his mother's kitchen and heard her discussing with the old house-servant where they could get a reliable substitute to help out now that the girl Thebedi had had a baby. For the first time since he was a small boy he came right into the kraal. It was eleven o'clock in the morning. The men were at work in the lands. He looked about him, urgently; the women turned away, each not wanting to be the one approached to point out where Thebedi lived. Thebedi appeared, coming slowly from the hut Njabulo had built in white man's style, with a tin chimney, and a proper window with glass panes set in straight as walls made of unfired bricks would allow. She greeted him with hands brought together and a token movement representing the respectful bob with which she was accustomed to acknowledge she was in the presence of his father or mother. He lowered his head under the doorway of her home and went in. He said, 'I want to see. Show me.'

She had taken the bundle off her back before she came out into the light to face him. She moved between the iron bedstead made up with Njabulo's checked blankets and the small wooden table where the pink plastic bath stood among food and kitchen pots, and picked up the bundle from the snugly blanketed grocer's box where it lay. The infant was asleep; she revealed the closed, pale, plump tiny face, with a bubble of spit at the corner of the mouth, the spidery pink hands stirring. She took off the woollen cap and the straight fine hair flew up after it in static electricity, showing gilded strands here and there. He said nothing. She was watching him as she had done when they were little, and the gang of children had trodden down a crop in their games or transgressed in some other way for which he, as the farmer's son, the white one among them, must intercede with the farmer. She disturbed the sleeping face by scratching or tickling gently at a cheek with one finger, and slowly the eyes opened, saw nothing, were still asleep, and then, awake, no longer narrowed, looked out at them, grey with yellowish flecks, his own hazel eyes.

He struggled for a moment with a grimace of tears, anger and self-pity. She could not put out her hand to him. He said, 'You haven't been near the house with it?'

She shook her head.

29

'Never?'

Again she shook her head.

'Don't take it out. Stay inside. Can't you take it away somewhere. You must give it to someone –'

She moved to the door with him.

He said, 'I'll see what I will do. I don't know.' And then he said: 'I feel like killing myself.'

Her eyes began to glow, to thicken with tears. For a moment there was the feeling between them that used to come when they were alone down at the river-bed.

He walked out.

Two days later, when his mother and father had left the farm for the day, he appeared again. The women were away on the lands, weeding, as they were employed to do as casual labour in summer; only the very old remained, propped up on the ground outside the huts in the flies and the sun. Thebedi did not ask him in. The child had not been well; it had diarrhoea. He asked where its food was. She said, 'The milk comes from me.' He went into Njabulo's house, where the child lay; she did not follow but stayed outside the door and watched without seeing an old crone who had lost her mind, talking to herself, talking to the fowls who ignored her.

She thought she heard small grunts from the hut, the kind of infant grunt that indicates a full stomach, a deep sleep. After a time, long or short she did not know, he came out and walked away with plodding stride (his father's gait) out of sight, towards his father's house.

The baby was not fed during the night and although she kept telling Njabulo it was sleeping, he saw for himself in the morning that it was dead. He comforted her with words and caresses. She did not cry but simply sat, staring at the door. Her hands were cold as dead chickens' feet to his touch.

Njabulo buried the little baby where farm workers were buried, in the place in the veld the farmer had given them. Some of the mounds had been left to weather away unmarked, others were covered with stones and a few had fallen wooden crosses.

He was going to make a cross but before it was finished the police came and dug up the grave and took away the dead baby: someone – one of the other labourers? their women? – had reported that the baby was almost white, that, strong and healthy, it had died suddenly after a visit by the farmer's son. Pathological tests on the infant corpse showed intestinal damage not always consistent with death by natural causes.

Thebedi went for the first time to the country town where Paulus had been to school, to give evidence at the preparatory examination into the charge of murder brought against him. She cried hysterically in the witness box, saying yes, yes (the gilt hoop ear-rings swung in her ears), she saw the accused pouring liquid into the baby's mouth. She said he had threatened to shoot her if she told anyone.

More than a year went by before, in that same town, the case was brought to trial. She came to Court with a new-born baby on her back. She wore gilt hoop ear-rings; she was calm; she said she had not seen what the white man did in the house.

Paulus Eysendyck said he had visited the hut but had not poisoned the child.

The Defence did not contest that there had been a love relationship between the accused and the girl, or that intercourse had taken place, but submitted there was no proof that the child was the accused's.

The judge told the accused there was strong suspicion against him but not enough proof that he had committed the crime. The Court could not accept the girl's evidence because it was clear she had committed perjury either at this trial or at the preparatory examination. There was the suggestion in the mind of the Court that she might be an accomplice in the crime; but, again insufficient proof.

The judge commended the honourable behaviour of the husband (sitting in court in a brown-and-yellow-quartered golf cap bought for Sundays) who had not rejected his wife and had 'even provided clothes for the unfortunate infant out of his slender means'.

The verdict on the accused was 'not guilty'.

The young white man refused to accept the congratulations of press and public and left the Court with his mother's raincoat shielding his face from photographers. His father said to the press, 'I will try and carry on as best I can to hold up my head in the district.'

Interviewed by the Sunday papers, who spelled her name in a variety of ways, the black girl, speaking in her own language, was quoted beneath her photograph: 'It was a thing of our childhood, we don't see each other any more.'

The Heart

V. S. Naipaul

WHEN THEY DECIDED that the only way to teach Hari to swim would be throw him into the sea, Hari dropped out of the sea scouts. Every Monday afternoon for a term he had put on the uniform, practised rowing on the school grounds, and learned to run up signals and make knots. The term before he had dropped out of the boy scouts, to avoid going to camp. At the school sports the term before that he had entered for all the races for the under-elevens, but when the time came he was too shy to strip (the emblem of his house had been fancifully embroidered on his vest by his mother), and he didn't run.

Hari was an only child. He was ten and had a weak heart. The doctors had advised against over-exertion and excitement, and Hari was unexercised and fat. He would have liked to play cricket, fancying himself as a fast bowler, but he was never picked for any of the form teams. He couldn't run quickly, he couldn't bowl, he couldn't bat, and he threw like a girl. He would also have liked to whistle, but he could only make hissing noises through his small plump lips. He had an almost Chinese passion for neatness. He wrote with a blotter below his hand and blotted each line as he wrote; he crossed out with the help of a ruler. His books were clean and unmarked, except on the fly-leaf, where his name had been written by his father. He would have passed unnoticed at school if he hadn't been so well provided with money. This made him unpopular and attracted bullies. His expensive fountain pens were always stolen; and he had learned to stay away from the tuck shop.

Most of the boys from Hari's district who went to the school used Jameson Street. Hari wished to avoid this street. The only way he could do this was to go down Rupert Street. And at the bottom of that street, just where he turned right, there was the house with the Alsatians.

The house stood on the right-hand corner and walking on the other side would have made his cowardice plain, to dogs and passers-by. The Alsatians bounded down from the veranda, barking, leapt against the wire fence and made it shake. Their paws touched the top of the fence and it always seemed to Hari that with a little effort they could jump right over. Sometimes a thin old lady with glasses and grey hair and an irritable expression limped out to the veranda and called in a squeaky voice to the Alsatians. At once they stopped barking, forgot Hari, ran up to the veranda and wagged their heavy tails, as though apologizing for the noise and at the same time asking to be congratulated. The old lady tapped them on the head and they continued to wag their tails; if she slapped them hard they moved away with their heads bowed, their tails between their legs, and lay down on the veranda, gazing out, blinking, their muzzles beneath their forelegs.

Hari envied the old lady her power over the dogs. He was glad when she came out; but he also felt ashamed of his own fear and weakness.

The city was full of unlicensed mongrels who barked in relay all through the day and night. Of these dogs Hari was not afraid. They were thin and starved and cowardly. To drive them away one had only to bend down as though reaching for a stone; it was a gesture the street dogs understood. But it didn't work with the Alsatians; it merely aggravated their fury.

Four times a day – he went home for lunch – Hari had to pass the Alsatians, hear their bark and breath, see their long white teeth, black lips and red tongues, see their eager, powerful bodies, taller than he when they leapt against the fence. He took his revenge on the street dogs. He picked up imaginary stones; and the street dogs always bolted.

When Hari asked for a bicycle he didn't mention the boys in Jameson Street or the Alsatians in Rupert Street. He spoke about the sun and his fatigue. His parents had misgivings about the bicycle, but Hari learned to ride without accident. And then, with the power of his bicycle, he was no longer afraid of the dogs in Rupert Street. The Alsatians seldom barked at passing cyclists. So Hari stopped in front of the house at the corner, and when the Alsatians ran down from the veranda he pretended to throw things at them until they were thoroughly enraged and their breath grew loud. Then he cycled slowly away, the Alsatians following along the fence to the end of the lot, growling with anger and frustration. Once, when the old lady came out, Hari pretended he had stopped only to tie his laces.

Hari's school was in a quiet, open part of the city. The streets were wide and there were no pavements, only broad, well-kept grass verges. The verges were not level; every few yards there were shallow trenches which drained off the water from the road. Hari liked cycling on the verges, gently rising and falling.

Late one Friday afternoon Hari was cycling back from school after a meeting of the Stamp Club (he had joined that after leaving the sea scouts and with the large collections and expensive albums given by his father he enjoyed a continuing esteem). It was growing dark as Hari cycled along the verge, falling and rising, looking down at the grass.

In a trench he saw the body of an Alsatian.

The bicycle rolled down into the trench and over the thick tail of the dog. The dog rose and, without looking at Hari, shook himself. Then Hari saw another Alsatian. And another. Steering to avoid them, he ran into more. They lay in the trenches and all over the verge. They were of varying colours; one was brown-black. Hari had not pedalled since he had seen the first dog and was now going so slowly he felt he was losing his balance. From behind him came a low, brief bark, like a sneeze. At this, energy returned to him. He rode on to the asphalt and it was only then, as though they too had just recovered from their surprise, that the Alsatians all rose and came after him. He pedalled, staring ahead, not looking at what was behind him or beside him. Three Alsatians, the brown-black one among them, were running abreast of his bicycle. Calmly, as he pedalled, Hari waited for their attack. But they only ran beside him, not barking. The bicycle hummed; the dogs' paws on the asphalt sounded like pigeons' feet on a tin roof. And then Hari felt that the savagery of the Alsatians was casual, without anger or malice: an evening gathering, an evening's pleasure. He fixed his eyes on the main road at the end, with the street lights just going on, the lighted trolley-buses, the motor-cars, the people.

Then he was there. The Alsatians had dropped behind. He didn't look for them. It was only when he was in the main road, with the trolley-poles sparking blue in the night already fallen, that he realized how frightened he had been, how close to painful death from the teeth of those happy dogs. His heart beat fast, from the exertion. Then he felt a sharp pain he had never known before. He gave a choked, deep groan and fell off the bicycle.

He spent a month in a nursing home and didn't go to school for the rest of that term. But he was well enough again when the new term began. It was decided that he should give up the bicycle; and his father changed his hours of work so that he could drive Hari to and from the school.

His birthday fell early that term, and when he was driven home from school in the afternoon his mother handed him a basket and said, 'Happy birthday!'

It was a puppy.

'He won't bite you,' his mother said. 'Touch him and see.'

'Let me see you touch him,' Hari said.

'You must touch him,' his mother said. 'He is yours. You must get him used to you. They are one-man dogs.'

He thought of the old lady with the squeaky voice and he held out his hand to the puppy. The puppy licked it and pressed a damp nose against it. Hari was tickled. He burst out laughing, felt the puppy's hair and the puppy rubbed against his hand; he passed his hand over the puppy's muzzle, then he lifted the puppy and the puppy licked his face and Hari was tickled into fresh laughter.

The puppy had small sharp teeth and liked to pretend that he was biting. Hari liked the feel of his teeth; there was friendliness in them, and soon there would be power. His power. 'They are one-man dogs,' his mother said.

He got his father to drive to school down Rupert Street. Sometimes he saw the Alsatians. Then he thought of his own dog, and felt protected and revenged. They drove up and down

37

the street with grass verges along which he had been chased by the Alsatians. But he never again saw any Alsatian there.

The puppy was always waiting when they got back home. His father drove right up to the gate and blew his horn. His mother came out to open the gate, and the puppy came out too, wagging his tail, leaping up against the car even as it moved. 'Hold him! Hold him!' Hari cried.

More than anything now he feared losing his dog.

He liked hearing his mother tell visitors about his love for the puppy. And he was given many books about dogs. He learned with sadness that they lived for only twelve years; so that when he was twenty-three, a man, he would have no dog. In the circumstances training seemed pointless, but the books all recommended training, and Hari tried it. The puppy responded with a languor Hari thought enchanting. At school he was moved almost to tears when they read the poem beginning 'A barking sound the shepherd hears'. He went to see the film *Lassie Come Home* and wept. From the film he realized that he had forgotten an important part of the puppy's training. And, to prevent his puppy eating food given by strangers, he dipped pieces of meat in peppersauce and left them about the yard.

The next day the puppy disappeared. Hari was distressed and felt guilty, but he got some consolation from the film; and when, less than a week later, the puppy returned, dirty, scratched and thinner, Hari embraced him and whispered the words of the film: 'You're my Lassie – my Lassie come home.'

He abandoned all training and was concerned only to see the puppy become healthy again. In the American comic books he read, dogs lived in dog-houses and ate from bowls marked DOG. Hari didn't approve of the dog-houses because they looked small and lonely; but he insisted that his mother should buy a bowl marked DOG.

When he came home for lunch one day she showed him a bowl on which DOG had been painted. Hari's father said he was too hot to eat and went upstairs; his mother followed. Before Hari ate he washed the bowl and filled it with dog-food.

He called for the puppy and displayed the bowl. The puppy jumped up, trying to get at the bowl.

Hari put the bowl down and the puppy, instantly ignoring Hari, ran to it. Disappointed, Hari squatted beside the puppy and waited for some sign of recognition. None came. The puppy ate noisily, seeming to catch his food for every chew. Hari passed his hand over the puppy's head.

The puppy, catching a mouthful of food, growled and shook his head.

Hari tried again.

With a sharper growl the puppy dropped the food he had in his mouth and snapped at Hari's hand. Hari felt teeth sinking into his flesh; he could sense the anger driving the teeth, the thought that finally held them back. When he looked at his hand he saw torn skin and swelling blobs of blood. The puppy was bent over the bowl again, catching and chewing, his eyes hard.

Hari seized the bowl marked DOG and threw it with his girl's throw out of the kitchen door. The puppy's growl abruptly ended. When the bowl disappeared he looked up at Hari, puzzled, friendly, his tail swinging slowly. Hari kicked hard at the puppy's muzzle and felt the tip of his shoe striking the bone. The puppy backed away to the door and looked at Hari with bewilderment.

'Come,' Hari said, his voice thick with saliva.

Swinging his tail briskly, the puppy came, passing his neat pink tongue over his black lips, still oily from the food. Hari held out his bitten hand. The puppy licked it clean of blood. Then Hari drove his shoe up against the puppy's belly. He kicked again, but the puppy had run whining out of the kitchen door, and Hari lost his balance and fell. Tears came to his eyes. His hands burned at those points where the puppy's teeth had sunk, and he could still feel the puppy's saliva on his hand, binding the skin.

He got up and went out of the kitchen. The puppy stood by the gate, watching him. Hari bent down, as though to pick up a stone. The puppy made no move. Hari picked up a pebble and flung it at the puppy. It was a clumsy throw and the pebble rose high. The puppy ran to catch it, missed, stopped and stared, his tail swinging, his ears erect, his mouth open. Hari threw another pebble. This one kept low and struck the puppy hard. The puppy whined and ran into the front garden. Hari followed. The puppy ran around the side of the house and hid among the anthurium lilies. Hari aimed one stone after another, and suddenly he had a sense of direction. Again and again he hit the puppy, who whined and ran until he was cornered below the narrow trellis with the Bleeding Heart vine. There he stood still, his eyes restless, his tail between his legs. From time to time he licked his lips. This action infuriated Hari. Blindly he threw stone after stone and the puppy ran from tangle to tangle of Bleeding Heart. Once he tried to rush past Hari, but the way was too narrow and Hari too quick. Hari caught him a drumming kick and he ran back to the corner, watching, faintly whining.

In a choked voice Hari said, 'Come.'

The puppy raised its ears.

Hari smiled and tried to whistle.

Hesitantly, his legs bent, his back curved, the puppy came. Hari stroked his head until the puppy stood erect. Then he held the muzzle with both his hands and squeezed it hard. The puppy yelped and pulled away.

'Hari!' He heard his mother's voice, 'Your father is nearly ready.'

He had had no lunch.

'I have no appetite,' Hari said. They were words his father often used.

She asked about the broken bowl and the food scattered about the yard.

'We were playing,' Hari said.

She saw his hand. 'Those animals don't know their own strength,' she said.

It was his resolve to get the puppy to allow himself to be stroked while eating. Every refusal had to be punished, by beating and stoning, imprisonment in the cupboard below the stairs or imprisonment behind the closed windows of the car, when that was available. Sometimes, Hari took the puppy's plate, led the puppy to the lavatory, emptied the plate into the toilet bowl and pulled the flush. Sometimes he threw the food into the yard; then he punished the puppy for eating off the ground. Soon he extended his judgement to all the puppy's actions, punishing those he thought unfriendly, disobedient or ungrateful. If the puppy didn't come to the gate when the car horn sounded, he was to be punished; if he didn't come when called, he was to be punished. Hari kept a careful check of the punishments he had to inflict because he could punish only when his parents were away or occupied, and he was therefore always behind-hand. He feared that the puppy might run away again; so he tied him at nights. And when his parents were about, Hari was enraged, as enraged as he had been by that licking of the oily lips, to see the puppy behaving as though unaware of the punishments to come: lying at his father's feet, yawning, curling himself into comfortable positions, or wagging his tail to greet Hari's mother. Sometimes, then, Hari stooped to pick up an imaginary stone, and the puppy ran out of the room. But there were also days when punishments were forgotten, for Hari knew that he controlled the puppy's power and made it an extension of his own, not only by his punishments but also by the complementary hold of affection.

Then came the triumph. The puppy, now almost a dog, attacked Hari one day and had to be pulled back by Hari's parents. 'You can never trust those dogs,' Hari's mother said, and the dog was permanently chained. For days, whenever he could get the chance, Hari beat the dog. One evening, when his parents were out, he beat the dog until it ceased to whine. Then, knowing he was alone, and wishing to test his strength and fear, he unchained the dog. The dog didn't attack, didn't growl. It

41

ran to hide among the anthurium lilies. And after that it allowed itself to be stroked while it ate.

Hari's birthday came again. He was given a Brownie 6-20 camera and wasted film on absurd subjects until his father suggested that a photograph should be taken of Hari and the dog. The dog didn't stand still; eventually they put its collar on and Hari held on to that and smiled for the camera.

Hari's father was busy that Friday and couldn't drive Hari home. Hari stayed at school for the meeting of the Stamp Club and took a taxi home. His father's car was in the drive. He called for the dog. It didn't come. Another punishment. His parents were in the small diningroom next to the kitchen; they sat down to tea. On the dining table Hari saw the yellow folder with the negatives and the prints. They had not come out well. The dog looked strained and awkward, not facing the camera; and Hari thought he himself looked very fat. He felt his parent's eyes on him as he went through the photographs. He turned over one photograph. On the back of it he saw, in his father's handwriting: *In memory of Rex*. Below that was the date.

'It was an accident,' his mother said, putting her arms around him. 'He ran out just as your father was driving in. It was an accident.'

Tears filled Hari's eyes. Sobbing, he stamped up the stairs.

'Mind, son,' his mother called, and Hari heard her say to his father, 'Go after him. His heart. His heart.'

The Second Hut

Doris Lessing

BEFORE THAT SEASON and his wife's illness, he had thought things could get no worse: until then, poverty had meant not to deviate further than snapping point from what he had been brought up to think of as a normal life.

Being a farmer (he had come to it late in life, in his forties) was the first test he had faced as an individual. Before he had always been supported, invisibly perhaps, but none the less strongly, by what his family expected of him. He had been a regular soldier, not an unsuccessful one, but his success had been at the cost of a continual straining against his own inclinations: and he did not know himself what his inclinations were. Something stubbornly unconforming kept him apart from his fellow officers. It was an inward difference: he did not think of himself as a soldier. Even in his appearance, square, close-bitten, disciplined, there had been a hint of softness, or of strain, showing itself in his smile, which was too quick, like the smile of a deaf person afraid of showing incomprehension, and in the anxious look of his eyes. After he left the army he quickly slackened into an almost slovenly carelessness of dress and carriage. Now, in his farm clothes there was nothing left to suggest the soldier. With a loose, stained felt hat on the back of his head, khaki shorts a little too long and too wide, sleeves flapping over spare brown arm, his wispy moustache hiding a strained, set mouth, Major Carruthers looked what he was, a gentleman farmer going to seed.

The house had that brave, worn appearance of those struggling to keep up appearances. It was a four-roomed shack, its red roof dulling to streaky brown. It was the sort of house an apprentice farmer builds as a temporary shelter till he can afford better. Inside, good but battered furniture stood over worn places in the rugs; the piano was out of tune and the notes stuck; the silver tea things from the big narrow house in England where his brother (a lawyer) now lived were used as ornaments, and inside were bits of paper, accounts, rubber rings, old corks.

The room where his wife lay, in a greenish sun-lanced gloom, was a place of seedy misery. The doctor said it was her heart;

and Major Carruthers knew this was true: she had broken down through heart-break over the conditions they lived in. She did not want to get better. The harsh light from outside was shut out with dark blinds, and she turned her face to the wall and lay there, hour after hour, inert and uncomplaining, in a stoicism of defeat nothing could penetrate. Even the children hardly moved her. It was as if she had said to herself: 'If I cannot have what I wanted for them, then I wash my hands of life.'

Sometimes Major Carruthers thought of her as she had been and was filled with uneasy wonder and with guilt. That pleasant conventional pretty English girl had been bred to make a perfect wife for the professional soldier she had imagined him to be, but chance had wrenched her on to this isolated African farm, into a life which she submitted herself to, as if it had nothing to do with her. For the first few years she had faced the struggle humorously, courageously: it was a sprightly attitude towards life, almost flirtatious, as a woman flirts lightly with a man who means nothing to her. As the house grew shabby, and the furniture, and her clothes could not be replaced; when she looked into the mirror and saw her drying, untidy hair and roughening face, she would give a quick high laugh and say, 'Dear me, the things one comes to!' She was facing this poverty as she would have faced, in England, poverty of a narrowing, but socially accepted kind. What she could not face was a different kind of fear; and Major Carruthers understood that too well, for it was now his own fear.

The two children were pale, fine-drawn creatures, almost transparent-looking in their thin nervous fairness, with the defensive and wary manners of the young who have been brought up to expect a better way of life than they enjoy. Their anxious solicitude wore on Major Carruthers' already over-sensitized nerves. Children had no right to feel the aching pity which showed on their faces whenever they looked at him. They were too polite, too careful, too scrupulous. When they went into their mother's room she grieved sorrowfully over them, and they submitted patiently to her emotion. All those weeks of the school holidays after she was taken ill, they moved about the farm like two strained and anxious ghosts, and whenever he saw them his sense of guilt throbbed like a wound. He was glad they were going back to school soon, for then – so he thought – it would be easier to manage. It was an intolerable strain, running the farm and coming back to the neglected house and the problems of food and clothing, and a sick wife who would not get better until he could offer her hope.

But when they had gone back, he found that after all, things were not much easier. He slept little, for his wife needed attention in the night; and he became afraid for his own health, worrying over what he ate and wore. He learnt to treat himself as if his health was not what he was, what made him, but something apart, a commodity like efficiency, which could be estimated in terms of money at the end of a season. His health stood between them and complete ruin; and soon there were medicine bottles beside his bed, as well as beside his wife's.

One day, while he was carefully measuring out tonics for himself in the bedroom, he glanced up and saw his wife's small reddened eyes staring incredulously but ironically at him over the bedclothes. 'What are you doing?' she asked.

'I need a tonic,' he explained awkwardly, afraid to worry her by explanations.

She laughed, for the first time in weeks; then the slack tears began welling under the lids, and she turned to the wall again.

He understood that some vision of himself had been destroyed, finally, for her. Now she was left with an ageing rather fussy gentleman, carefully measuring medicine after meals. But he did not blame her; he never had blamed her; not even though he knew her illness was a failure of will. He patted her cheek uncomfortably, and said: 'It wouldn't do for me to get run down, would it?' Then he adjusted the curtains over the windows to shut out a streak of dancing light that threatened to fall over her face, set a glass nearer to her hand, and went out to arrange for her tray of slops to be carried in.

Then he took, in one swift, painful movement, as if he were leaping over an obstacle, the decision he had known for weeks he must take sooner or later. With a straightening of his shoulders, an echo from his soldier past, he took on the strain of an extra burden: he must get an assistant, whether he liked it or not.

So much did he shrink from any self-exposure, that he did not even consider advertising. He sent a note by native bearer to his neighbour, a few miles off, asking that it should be spread abroad that he was wanting help. He knew he would not have to wait long. It was 1931, in the middle of a slump, and there was unemployment, which was a rare thing for this new, sparsely-populated country.

He wrote the following to his two sons at boarding-school:

I expect you will be surprised to hear I'm getting another man on the place. Things are getting a bit too much, and as I plan to plant a bigger acreage of maize this year, I thought it would need two of us. Your mother is better this week, on the whole, so I think things are looking up. She is looking forward to your next holidays, and asks me to say she will write soon. Between you and me, I don't think she's up to writing at the moment. It will soon be getting cold, I think, so if you need any clothes, let me know, and I'll see what I can do . . .

A week later, he sat on the little veranda, towards evening, smoking, when he saw a man coming through the trees on a bicycle. He watched him closely, already trying to form an estimate of his character by the tests he had used all his life: the width between the eyes, the shape of the skull, the way the legs were set on to the body. Although he had been taken in a dozen times, his belief in these methods never wavered. He was an easy prey for any trickster, lending money he never saw again, taken in by professional adventurers who (it seemed to him, measuring others by his own decency and the quick warmth he felt towards people) were the essence of gentlemen. He used to say that being a gentleman was a question of instinct: one could not mistake a gentleman.

As the visitor stepped off his bicycle and wheeled it to the veranda, Major Carruthers saw he was young, thirty perhaps, sturdily built, with enormous strength in the thick arms and shoulders. His skin was burnt a healthy orange-brown colour. His close hair, smooth as the fur of an animal, reflected no light. His obtuse, generous features were set in a round face, and the eyes were pale grey, nearly colourless.

Major Carruthers instinctively dropped his standards of value as he looked, for this man was an Afrikander, and thus came into an outside category. It was not that he disliked him for it, although his father had been killed in the Boer War, but he had never had anything to do with the Afrikaans people before, and his knowledge of them was hearsay, from Englishmen who had the old prejudice. But he liked the look of the man: he liked the honest and straightforward face.

As for Van Heerden, he immediately recognized his traditional enemy, and his inherited dislike was strong. For a moment he appeared obstinate and wary. But they needed each other too badly to nurse old hatreds, and Van Heerden sat down when he was asked, though awkwardly, suppressing reluctance, and began drawing patterns in the dust with a piece of straw he had held between his lips.

Major Carruthers did not need to wonder about the man's circumstances: his quick acceptance of what were poor terms spoke of a long search for work.

He said scrupulously: 'I know the salary is low and the living quarters are bad, even for a single man. I've had a patch of bad luck, and I can't afford more. I'll quite understand if you refuse.'

'What are the living quarters?' asked Van Heerden. His was the rough voice of the uneducated Afrikander: because he was uncertain where the accent should fall in each sentence, his speech had a wavering, halting sound, though his look and manner were direct enough.

Major Carruthers pointed ahead of them. Before the house

the bush sloped gently down to the fields. 'At the foot of the hill there's a hut I've been using as a storehouse. It's quite well-built. You can put up a place for a kitchen.'

Van Heerden rose. 'Can I see it?'

They set off. It was not far away. The thatched hut stood in uncleared bush. Grass grew to the walls and reached up to meet the slanting thatch. Trees mingled their branches overhead. It was round, built of poles and mud and with a stamped dung floor. Inside there was a stale musty smell because of the ants and beetles that had been at the sacks of grain. The one window was boarded over, and it was quite dark. In the confusing shafts of light from the door, a thick sheet of felted spider web showed itself, like a curtain halving the interior, as full of small flies and insects as a butcher-bird's cache. The spider crouched, vast and glittering, shaking gently, glaring at them with small red eyes, from the centre of the web. Van Heerden did what Major Carruthers would have died rather than do: he tore the web across with his bare hands, crushed the spider between his fingers, and brushed them lightly against the walls to free them from the clinging silky strands and the sticky mush of insect-body.

'It will do fine,' he announced.

He would not accept the invitation to a meal, thus making it clear this was merely a business arrangement. But he asked, politely (hating that he had to beg a favour), for a month's salary in advance. Then he set off on his bicycle to the store, ten miles off, to buy what he needed for his living.

Major Carruthers went back to his sick wife with a burdened feeling, caused by his being responsible for another human being having to suffer such conditions. He could not have the man in the house: the idea came into his head and was quickly dismissed. They had nothing in common, they would make each other uncomfortable – that was how he put it to himself. Besides, there wasn't really any room. Underneath, Major Carruthers knew that if his new assistant had been an Englishman, with the same upbringing, he would have found a corner in his house and a welcome as a friend. Major Carruthers threw off these thoughts: he had enough to worry him without taking on another man's problems.

A person who had always hated the business of organization, which meant dividing responsibility with others, he found it hard to arrange with Van Heerden how the work was to be done. But as the Dutchman was good with cattle, Major Carruthers handed over all the stock on the farm to his care, thus relieving his mind of its most nagging care, for he was useless with beasts, and knew it. So they began, each knowing exactly where they stood. Van Heerden would make laconic reports at the end of each week, in the manner of an expert foreman reporting to a boss ignorant of technicalities – and Major Carruthers accepted this attitude, for he liked to respect people, and it was easy to respect Van Heerden's inspired instinct for animals.

For a few weeks Major Carruthers was almost happy. The fear of having to apply for another loan to his brother – worse, asking for the passage money to England and a job, thus justifying his family's belief in him as a failure, was pushed away; for while taking on a manager did not in itself improve things, it was an action, a decision, and there was nothing that he found more dismaying than decisions. The thought of his family in England, and particularly his elder brother, pricked him into slow burning passions of resentment. His brother's letters galled him so that he had grown to hate mail-days. They were crisp, affectionate letters, without condescension, but about money, bank-drafts, and insurance policies. Major Carruthers did not see life like that. He had not written to his brother for over a year. His wife, when she was well, wrote once a week, in the spirit of one propitiating fate.

Even she seemed cheered by the manager's coming; she sensed her husband's irrational lightness of spirit during that short time. She stirred herself to ask about the farm; and he began to see that her interest in living would revive quickly if her sort of life came within reach again.

But some two months after Van Heerden's coming, Major Carruthers was walking along the farm road towards his lands, when he was astonished to see, disappearing into the bushes, a small flaxen-haired boy. He called, but the child froze as an animal freezes, flattening himself against the foliage. At last, since he could get no reply, Major Carruthers approached the child, who dissolved backwards through the trees, and followed him up the path to the hut. He was very angry, for he knew what he would see.

He had not been to the hut since he handed it over to Van Heerden. Now there was a clearing, and amongst the stumps of trees and the flattened grass, were half a dozen children, each as tow-headed as the first, with that bleached sapless look common to white children in the tropics who have been subjected to too much sun.

A lean-to had been built against the hut. It was merely a roof of beaten petrol tins, patched together like cloth with wire and nails and supported on two unpeeled sticks. There, holding a cooking pot over an open fire that was dangerously close to the thatch, stood a vast slatternly woman. She reminded him of a sow among her litter, as she lifted her head, the children crowding about her, and stared at him suspiciously from pale and white-lashed eyes.

'Where is your husband?' he demanded.

She did not answer. Her suspicion deepened into a glare of hate: clearly she knew no English.

Striding furiously to the door of the hut, he saw that it was crowded with two enormous native-style beds: strips of hide stretched over wooden poles embedded in the mud of the floor. What was left of the space was heaped with the stained and broken belongings of the family. Major Carruthers strode off in search of Van Heerden. His anger was now mingled with the shamed discomfort of trying to imagine what it must be to live in such squalor.

Fear rose high in him. For a few moments he inhabited the landscape of his dreams, a grey country full of sucking menace, where he suffered what he would not allow himself to think of while awake: the grim poverty that could overtake him if his luck did not turn, and if he refused to submit to his brother and return to England.

Walking through the fields, where the maize was now waving over his head, pale gold with a froth of white, the sharp dead leaves scything crisply against the wind, he could see nothing but that black foetid hut and the pathetic futureless children. That was the lowest he could bring his own children to! He felt moorless, helpless, afraid: his sweat ran cold on him. And he did not hesitate in his mind; driven by fear and anger, he told himself to be hard; he was searching in his mind for the words with which he would dismiss the Dutchman who had brought his worst nightmares to life, on his own farm, in glaring daylight, where they were inescapable.

He found him with a screaming rearing young ox that was being broken to the plough, handling it with his sure understanding of animals. At a cautious distance stood the natives who were assisting; but Van Heerden, fearless and purposeful, was fighting the beast at close range. He saw Major Carruthers, let go the plunging horn he held, and the ox shot away backwards, roaring with anger, into the crowd of natives, who gathered loosely about it with sticks, and stones to prevent it running away altogether.

Van Heerden stood still, wiping the sweat off his face, still grinning with the satisfaction of the fight, waiting for his employer to speak.

'Van Heerden,' said Major Carruthers, without preliminaries, 'why didn't you tell me you had a family?'

As he spoke the Dutchman's face changed, first flushing into guilt, then setting hard and stubborn. 'Because I've been out of work for a year, and I knew you would not take me if I told you.'

The two men faced each other, Major Carruthers tall, fly-away, shambling, bent with responsibility; Van Heerden stiff and defiant. The natives remained about the ox, to prevent its escape – for them this was a brief intermission in the real work of the farm – and their shouts mingled with the incessant bellowing. It was a hot day; Van Heerden wiped the sweat from his eyes with the back of his hand.

'You can't keep a wife and all those children here – how many children?'

'Nine.'

Major Carruthers thought of his own two, and his perpetual dull ache of worry over them; and his heart became grieved for Van Heerden. Two children, with all the trouble over everything they ate and wore and thought, and what would become of them, were too great a burden; how did this man, with nine, manage to look so young?

'How old are you?' he asked abruptly, in a different tone.

'Thirty-four,' said Van Heerden, suspiciously, unable to understand the direction Major Carruthers followed.

The only marks on his face were sun-creases; it was impossible to think of him as the father of nine children and the husband of that terrible broken-down woman. As Major Carruthers gazed at him, he became conscious of the strained lines on his own face, and tried to loosen himself, because he took so badly what this man bore so well.

'You can't keep a wife and children in such conditions.'

'We were living in a tent in the bush on mealie meal and what I shot for nine months, and that was through the wet season,' said Van Heerden drily.

Major Carruthers knew he was beaten. 'You've put me in a false position, Van Heerden,' he said angrily. 'You know I can't afford to give you more money. I don't know where I'm going to find my own children's school fees, as it is. I told you the position when you came. I can't afford to keep a man with such a family.'

'Nobody can afford to have me either,' said Van Heerden sullenly.

'How can I have you living on my place in such a fashion? Nine children! They should be at school. Didn't you know there is a law to make them go to school? Hasn't anybody been to see you about them?'

'They haven't got me yet. They won't get me unless someone tells them.'

Against this challenge, which was also unwilling appeal, Major Carruthers remained silent, until he said brusquely:

'Remember, I'm not responsible.' And he walked off, with all the appearance of anger.

Van Heerden looked after him, his face puzzled. He did not know whether or not he had been dismissed. After a few moments he moistened his dry lips with his tongue, wiped his hand again over his eyes, and turned back to the ox. Looking over his shoulder from the edge of the field, Major Carruthers could see his wiry, stocky figure leaping and bending about the ox whose bellowing made the whole farm ring with anger.

Major Carruthers decided, once and for all, to put the family out of his mind. But they haunted him; he even dreamed of them; and he could not determine whether it was his own or the Dutchman's children who filled his sleep with fear.

It was a very busy time of the year. Harassed, like all his fellow-farmers, by labour difficulties, apportioning out the farm tasks was a daily problem. All day his mind churned slowly over the necessities: this fencing was urgent, that field must be reaped at once. Yet, in spite of this, he decided it was his plain duty to build a second hut beside the first. It would do no more than take the edge off the discomfort of that miserable family, but he knew he could not rest until it was built.

Just as he had made up his mind and was wondering how the thing could be managed, the bossboy came to him, saying that unless the Dutchman went, he and his friends would leave the farm.

'Why?' asked Major Carruthers, knowing what the answer would be. Van Heerden was a hard worker, and the cattle were improving week by week under his care, but he could not handle natives. He shouted at them, lost his temper, treated them like dogs. There was continual friction.

'Dutchmen are no good,' said the bossboy simply, voicing the hatred of the black man for that section of the white people he considers his most brutal oppressors.

Now, Major Carruthers was proud that at a time when most farmers were forced to buy labour from the contractors, he was able to attract sufficient voluntary labour to run his farm. He was a good employer, proud of his reputation for fair dealing. Many of his natives had been with him for years, taking a few months off occasionally for a rest in their kraals, but always returning to him. His neighbours were complaining of the sullen attitude of their labourers: so far Major Carruthers had kept this side of that form of passive resistance which could ruin a farmer. It was walking on a knife-edge, but his simple human relationship with his workers was his greatest asset as a farmer, and he knew it.

He stood and thought, while his bossboy, who had been on this farm twelve years, waited for a reply. A great deal was at stake. For a moment Major Carruthers thought of dismissing the Dutchman; he realized he could not bring himself to do it: what would happen to all those children? He decided on a course which was repugnant to him. He was going to appeal to his employee's pity.

'I have always treated you square?' he asked. 'I've always helped you when you were in trouble?'

The bossboy immediately and warmly assented.

'You know that my wife is ill, and that I'm having a lot of trouble just now? I don't want the Dutchman to go, just now when the work is so heavy. I'll speak to him, and if there is any more trouble with the men, then come to me and I'll deal with it myself.'

It was a glittering blue day, with a chill edge on the air, that stirred Major Carruthers' thin blood as he stood, looking in appeal into the sullen face of the native. All at once, feeling the fresh air wash along his cheeks, watching the leaves shake with a ripple of gold on the trees down the slope, he felt superior to his difficulties, and able to face anything. 'Come,' he said, with his rare, diffident smile. 'After all these years, when we have been working together for so long, surely you can do this for me. It won't be for very long.'

He watched the man's face soften in response to his own; and wondered at the unconscious use of the last phrase, for there was no reason, on the face of things, why the situation should not continue as it was for a very long time.

They began laughing together; and separated cheerfully; the African shaking his head ruefully over the magnitude of the sacrifice asked of him, thus making the incident into a joke; and he dived off into the bush to explain the position to his fellow-workers.

Repressing a strong desire to go after him, to spend the lovely fresh day walking for pleasure, Major Carruthers went into his wife's bedroom, inexplicably confident and walking like a young man.

She lay as always, face to the wall, her protruding shoulders visible beneath the cheap pink bed-jacket he had bought for her illness. She seemed neither better nor worse. But as she turned her head, his buoyancy infected her a little; perhaps, too, she was conscious of the exhilarating day outside her gloomy curtains.

What kind of a miraculous release was she waiting for? he wondered, as he delicately adjusted her sheets and pillows and laid his hand gently on her head. Over the bony cage of the skull, the skin was papery and blueish. What was she thinking? He had a vision of her brain as a small frightened animal pulsating under his fingers.

With her eyes still closed, she asked in her querulous thin voice: 'Why don't you write to George?'

Involuntarily his fingers contracted on her hair, causing her to start and to open her reproachful, red-rimmed eyes. He waited for her usual appeal: the children, my health, our future. But she sighed and remained silent, still loyal to the man she had imagined she was marrying; and he could feel her thinking: *the lunatic stiff pride of men.*

Understanding that for her it was merely a question of waiting for his defeat, as her deliverance, he withdrew his hand, in dislike of her, saying: 'Things are not as bad as that yet.' The cheerfulness of his voice was genuine, holding still the courage and hope instilled into him by the bright day outside.

'Why, what has happened?' she asked swiftly, her voice suddenly strong, looking at him in hope.

'Nothing,' he said; and the depression settled down over him again. Indeed, nothing had happened; and his confidence was a trick of the nerves. Soberly he left the bedroom, thinking: I must get that well built; and when that is done, I must do the drains and then . . . He was thinking, too, that all these things must wait for the second hut.

Oddly, the comparatively small problem of that hut occupied his mind during the next few days. A slow and careful man, he set milestones for himself and overtook them one by one.

Since Christmas the labourers had been working a seven-day week, in order to keep ahead in the race against the weeds. They resented it, of course, but that was the custom. Now that the maize was grown, they expected work to slack off, they expected their Sundays to be restored to them. To ask even half a dozen of them to sacrifice their weekly holiday for the sake of the hated Dutchman might precipitate a crisis. Major Carruthers took his time, stalking his opportunity like a hunter, until one evening he was talking with his bossboy as man to man, about farm problems; but when he broached the subject of a hut, Major Carruthers saw that it would be as he feared: the man at once turned stiff and unhelpful. Suddenly impatient, he said: 'It must be done next Sunday. Six men could finish it in a day, if they worked hard.'

The black man's glance became veiled and hostile. Responding to the authority in the voice he replied simply: 'Yes, baas.' He was accepting the order from above, and refusing responsibility: his cooperation was switched off; he had become a machine for transmitting orders. Nothing exasperated Major Carruthers more than when this happened. He said sternly:

'I'm not having any nonsense. If that hut isn't built, there'll be trouble.'

'Yes, baas,' said the bossboy again. He walked away, stopped some natives who were coming off the fields with their hoes over their shoulders, and transmitted the order in a neutral voice. Major Carruthers saw them glance at him in fierce antagonism; then they turned away their heads, and walked off, in a group, towards their compound.

It would be all right, he thought, in disproportionate relief. It would be difficult to say exactly what it was he feared, for the question of the hut had loomed so huge in his mind that he was beginning to feel an almost superstitious foreboding. Driven downwards through failure after failure, fate was becoming real to him as a cold malignant force; the careful balancing of unfriendly probabilities that underlay all his planning had developed in him an acute sensitivity to the future; and he had learned to respect his dreams and omens. Now he wondered at the strength of his desire to see that hut built, and whatever danger it represented behind him.

He went to the clearing to find Van Heerden and tell him what had been planned. He found him sitting on a candlebox in the doorway of the hut, playing good-humouredly with his children, as if they had been puppies, tumbling them over, snapping his fingers in their faces, and laughing outright with boyish exuberance when one little boy squared up his fists at him in a moment of temper against this casual, almost contemptuous treatment of them. Major Carruthers heard that boyish laugh with amazement; he looked blankly at the young Dutchman, and then from him to his wife, who was standing, as usual, over a petrol tin that balanced on the small fire. A smell of meat and pumpkin filled the clearing. The woman seemed to Major Carruthers less a human being than the expression of an elemental, irrepressible force: he saw her, in her vast sagging fleshiness, with her slow stupid face, her instinctive responses to her children, whether for affection or temper, as the symbol of fecundity, a strong, irresistible heave of matter. She frightened him. He turned his eyes from her and explained to Van Heerden that a second hut would be built here, beside the existing one.

Van Heerden was pleased. He softened into quick confiding friendship. He looked doubtfully behind him at the small hut that sheltered eleven human beings, and said that it was really not easy to live in such a small space with so many children. He glanced at the children, cuffing them affectionately as he spoke, smiling like a boy. He was proud of his family, of his own capacity for making children: Major Carruthers could see that. Almost, he smiled; then he glanced through the doorway at the grey squalor of the interior and hurried off, resolutely preventing himself from dwelling on the repulsive facts that such close-packed living implied.

The next Saturday evening he and Van Heerden paced the clearing with tape measure and spirit level, determining the area of the new hut. It was to be a large one. Already the sheaves of thatching grass had been stacked ready for next day, shining brassily in the evening sun; and the thorn poles for the walls lay about the clearing, stripped of bark, the smooth inner wood showing white as kernels.

Major Carruthers was waiting for the natives to come up from the compound for the building before daybreak that Sunday. He was there even before the family woke, afraid that without his presence something might go wrong. He feared the Dutchman's temper because of the labourers' sulky mood.

He leaned against a tree, watching the bush come awake, while the sky flooded slowly with light, and the birds sang about him. The hut was, for a long time, silent and dark. A sack hung crookedly over the door, and he could glimpse huddled shapes within. It seemed to him horrible, a stinking kennel shrinking ashamedly to the ground away from the wide hall of fresh blue sky. Then a child came out, and another; soon they were spilling out of the doorway, in their little rags of dresses, or hitching khaki pants up over the bony jut of a hip. They smiled shyly at him, offering him friendship. Then came the woman, moving sideways to ease herself through the narrow door-frame – she was so huge it was almost a fit. She lumbered slowly, thick and stupid with sleep, over to the cold fire, raising her arms in a yawn, so that wisps of dull yellow hair fell over her shoulders and her dark slack dress lifted in creases under her neck. Then she saw Major Carruthers and smiled at him. For the first time he saw her as a human being and not as something fatally ugly. There was something shy, yet frank, in that smile; so that he could imagine the strong, laughing adolescent girl, with the frank, inviting, healthy sensuality of the young Dutchwoman – so she had been when she married Van Heerden. She stooped painfully to stir up the ashes, and soon the fire spurted up under the leaning patch of tin roof. For a while Van Heerden did not appear; neither did the natives who were supposed to be here a long while since; Major Carruthers continued to lean against a tree, smiling at the children, who nevertheless kept their distance from him unable to play naturally because of his presence there, smiling at Mrs Van Heerden who was throwing handfuls of mealie meal into a petrol tin of boiling water, to make native-style porridge.

It was just on eight o'clock, after two hours of impatient waiting, that the labourers filed up the bushy incline, with the axes and picks over their shoulders, avoiding his eyes. He pressed down his anger: after all it was Sunday, and they had had no day off for weeks; he could not blame them.

They began by digging the circular trench that would hold the wall poles. As their picks rang out on the pebbly ground, Van Heerden came out of the hut, pushing aside the dangling sack with one hand and pulling up his trousers with the other, yawning broadly, then smiling at Major Carruthers apologetically. 'I've had my sleep out,' he said; he seemed to think his employer might be angry.

Major Carruthers stood close over the workers, wanting it to be understood by them and by Van Heerden that he was responsible. He was too conscious of their resentment, and knew that they would scamp the work if possible. If the hut was to be completed as planned, he would need all his tact and good-humour. He stood there patiently all morning, watching the thin sparks flash up as the picks swung into the flinty earth. Van Heerden lingered nearby, unwilling to be thus publicly superseded in the responsibility for his own dwelling in the eyes of the natives.

When they flung their picks and went to fetch the poles, they did so with a side glance at Major Carruthers, challenging him to say the trench was not deep enough. He called them back, laughingly, saying: 'Are you digging for a dog-kennel then, and not a hut for a man?' One smiled unwillingly in response; the others sulked. Perfunctorily they deepened the trench to the very minimum that Major Carruthers was likely to pass. By noon, the poles were leaning drunkenly in place, and the natives were stripping the binding from beneath the bark of nearby trees. Long fleshy strips of fibre, rose-coloured and apricot and yellow, lay tangled over the grass, and the wounded trees showed startling red gashes around the clearing. Swiftly the poles were laced together with this natural rope, so that when the frame was complete it showed up against green trees and sky like a slender gleaming white cage, interwoven lightly with rosy-yellow. Two natives climbed on top to bind the roof poles into their conical shape, while the others stamped a slushy mound of sand and earth to form plaster for the walls. Soon they stopped – the rest could wait until after the midday break.

Worn out by the strain of keeping the balance between the fiery Dutchman and the resentful workers, Major Carruthers went off home to eat. He had one and a half hour's break. He finished his meal in ten minutes, longing to be able to sleep for once till he woke naturally. His wife was dozing, so he lay down on the other bed and at once dropped off to sleep himself. When he woke it was long after the time he had set himself. It was after three. He rose in a panic and strode to the clearing, in the grip of one of his premonitions.

There stood the Dutchman, in a flaring temper, shouting at the natives who lounged in front of him, laughing openly.

They had only just returned to work. As Major Carruthers approached, he saw Van Heerden using his open palms in a series of quick swinging slaps against their faces, knocking them sideways against each other: it was as if he were cuffing his own children in a fit of anger. Major Carruthers broke into a run, erupting into the group before anything else could happen. Van Heerden fell back on seeing him. He was beef-red with fury. The natives were bunched together, on the point of throwing down their tools and walking off the job.

'Get back to work,' snapped Major Carruthers to the men: and to Van Heerden: 'I'm dealing with this.' His eyes were an appeal to recognize the need for tact, but Van Heerden stood squarely there in front of him, on planted legs, breathing heavily. 'But Major Carruthers . . .' he began, implying that as a white man, with his employer not there, it was right that he should take the command. 'Do as I say,' said Major Carruthers. Van Heerden, with a deadly look at his opponents, swung on his heel and marched off into the hut. The slapping swing of the grainbag was as if a door had been slammed. Major Carruthers turned to the natives. 'Get on,' he ordered briefly, in a calm decisive voice. There was a moment of uncertainty. Then they picked up their tools and went to work.

Some laced the framework of the roof; others slapped the mud on to the walls. This business of plastering was usually a festival, with laughter and raillery, for there were gaps between the poles, and a handful of mud could fly through a space into the face of a man standing behind: the thing could become a game, like children playing snowballs. Today there was no pretence at good-humour. When the sun went down the men picked up their tools and filed off into the bush without a glance at Major Carruthers. The work had not prospered. The grass was laid untidily over the roof-frame, still uncut and reaching to the ground in long swatches. The first layer of mud had been unevenly flung on. It would be a shabby building.

'His own fault,' thought Major Carruthers, sending his slow, tired blue glance to the hut where the Dutchman was still cherishing the seeds of wounded pride. Next day, when Major Carruthers was in another part of the farm, the Dutchman got his own back in a fine flaming scene with the ploughboys: they came to complain to the bossboy, but not to Major Carruthers. This made him uneasy. All that week he waited for fresh complaints about the Dutchman's behaviour. So much was he keyed up, waiting for the scene between himself and a grudging bossboy, that when nothing happened his apprehensions deepened into a deep foreboding.

The building was finished the following Sunday. The floors were stamped hard with new dung, the thatch trimmed, and the walls grained smooth. Another two weeks must elapse before the family could move in, for the place smelled of damp. They were weeks of worry for Major Carruthers. It was unnatural for the Africans to remain passive and sullen under the Dutchman's handling of them, and especially when they knew he was on their side. There was something he did not like in the way they would not meet his eyes and in the over-polite attitude of the bossboy.

The beautiful clear weather that he usually loved so much, May weather, sharpened by cold, and crisp under deep clear skies, pungent with gusts of wind from the drying leaves and grasses of the veld, was spoilt for him this year: something was going to happen.

When the family eventually moved in, Major Carruthers became discouraged because the building of the hut had represented such trouble and worry, while now things seemed hardly better than before: what was the use of two small round huts for a family of eleven? But Van Heerden was very pleased, and expressed his gratitude in a way that moved Major Carruthers deeply: unable to show feeling himself, he was grateful when others did, so relieving him of the burden of his shyness. There was a ceremonial atmosphere on the evening when one of the great sagging beds was wrenched out of the floor of the first hut and its legs plastered down newly into the second hut.

That very same night he was awakened towards dawn by

voices calling to him from outside his window. He started up, knowing that whatever he had dreaded was here, glad that the tension was over. Outside the back door stood his bossboy, holding a hurricane lamp which momentarily blinded Major Carruthers.

'The hut is on fire.'

Blinking his eyes, he turned to look. Away in the darkness flames were lapping over the trees, outlining branches so that as a gust of wind lifted them patterns of black leaves showed clear and fine against the flowing red light of the fire. The veld was illuminated with a fitful plunging glare. The two men ran off into the bush down the rough road, towards the blaze.

The clearing was lit up, as bright as morning, when they arrived. On the roof of the first hut squatted Van Heerden, lifting tins of water from a line of natives below, working from the water-butt, soaking the thatch to prevent it catching the flames from the second hut that was only a few yards off. That was a roaring pillar of fire. Its frail skeleton was still erect, but twisting and writhing incandescently within its envelope of flame, and it collapsed slowly as he came up, subsiding in a crash of sparks.

'The children,' gasped Major Carruthers to Mrs Van Heerden, who was watching the blaze fatalistically from where she sat on a scattered bundle of bedding, the tears soaking down her face, her arms tight round a swathed child.

As he spoke she opened the cloths to display the smallest infant. A swathe of burning grass from the roof had fallen across its head and shoulders. He sickened as he looked, for there was nothing but raw charred flesh. But it was alive: the limbs still twitched a little.

'I'll get the car and we'll take it in to the doctor.'

He ran out of the clearing and fetched the car. As he tore down the slope back again he saw he was still in his pyjamas, and when he gained the clearing for the second time, Van Heerden was climbing down from the roof, which dripped water as if there had been a storm. He bent over the burnt child.

'Too late,' he said.

'But it's still alive.'

Van Heerden almost shrugged; he appeared dazed. He continually turned his head to survey the glowing heap that had so recently sheltered his children. He licked his lips with a quick unconscious movement, because of their burning dryness. His face was grimed with smoke and inflamed from the great heat, so that his young eyes showed startlingly clear against the black skin.

'Get into the car,' said Major Carruthers to the woman. She automatically moved towards the car, without looking at her husband, who said: 'But it's too late, man.'

Major Carruthers knew the child would die, but his protest against the waste and futility of the burning expressed itself in this way: that everything must be done to save this life, even against hope. He started the car and slid off down the hill. Before they had gone half a mile he felt his shoulder plucked from behind, and, turning, saw the child was now dead. He reversed the car into the dark bush off the road, and drove back to the clearing. Now the woman had begun wailing, a soft monotonous, almost automatic sound that kept him tight in his seat, waiting for the next cry.

The fire was now a dark heap, fanning softly to a glowing red as the wind passed over it. The children were standing in a half-circle, gazing fascinated at it. Van Heerden stood near them, laying his hands gently, restlessly, on their heads and shoulders, reassuring himself of their existence there, in the flesh and living, beside him.

Mrs Van Heerden got clumsily out of the car, still wailing, and disappeared into the hut, clutching the bundled dead child.

Feeling out of place among that bereaved family, Major Carruthers went up to his house, where he drank cup after cup of tea, holding himself tight and controlled, conscious of over-strained nerves.

Then he stooped into his wife's room, which seemed small and dark, and airless. The cave of a sick animal, he thought, in disgust; then, ashamed of himself, he returned out of doors, where the sky was filling with light. He sent a message for the bossboy, and waited for him in a condition of tensed anger.

When the man came Major Carruthers asked immediately: 'Why did that hut burn?'

The bossboy looked at him straight and said: 'How should I know?' Then, after a pause, with guileful innocence: 'It was the fault of the kitchen, too close to the thatch.'

Major Carruthers glared at him, trying to wear down the straight gaze with his own accusing eyes.

'That hut must be rebuilt at once. It must be rebuilt today.'

The bossboy seemed to say that it was a matter of indifference to him whether it was rebuilt or not. 'I'll go and tell the others,' he said, moving off.

'Stop' barked Major Carruthers. Then he paused, frightened, not so much at his rage, but his humiliation and guilt. He had foreseen it! He had foreseen it all! And yet, that thatch could so easily have caught alight from the small incautious fire that sent up sparks all day so close to it.

Almost, he burst out in wild reproaches. Then he pulled himself together and said: 'Get away from me.' What was the use? He knew perfectly well that one of the Africans whom Van Heerden had kicked or slapped or shouted at had fired that hut; no one could ever prove it.

He stood quite still, watching his bossboy move off, tugging at the long wisps of his moustache in frustrated anger.

And what would happen now?

He ordered breakfast, drank a cup of tea, and spoilt a piece of toast. Then he glanced in again at his wife, who would sleep for a couple of hours yet.

Again tugging fretfully at his moustache, Major Carruthers set off for the clearing.

Everything was just as it had been, though the pile of black débris looked low and shabby now that morning had come and heightened the wild colour of sky and bush. The children were playing nearby, their hands and faces black, their rags of clothing black – everything seemed patched and smudged with black, and on one side the trees hung withered and grimy and the soil was hot underfoot.

Van Heerden leaned against the framework of the first hut. He looked subdued and tired, but otherwise normal. He greeted Major Carruthers, and did not move.

'How is your wife?' asked Major Carruthers. He could hear a moaning sound from inside the hut.

'She's doing well.'

Major Carruthers imagined her weeping over the dead child; and said: 'I'll take your baby into town for you and arrange for the funeral.'

Van Heerden said: 'I've buried her already.' He jerked his thumb at the bush behind them.

'Didn't you register its birth?'

Van Heerden shook his head. His gaze challenged Major Carruthers as if to say: Who's to know if no one tells them? Major Carruthers could not speak: he was held in silence by the thought of that charred little body, huddled into a packing-case or wrapped in a piece of cloth, thrust into the ground, at the mercy of wild animals or of white ants.

'Well, one comes and another goes,' said Van Heerden at last, slowly, reaching out for philosophy as a comfort, while his eyes filled with rough tears.

Major Carruthers stared: he could not understand. At last the meaning of the words came into him, and he heard the moaning from the hut with a new understanding.

The idea had never entered his head; it had been a complete failure of the imagination. If nine children, why not ten? Why not fifteen, for that matter, or twenty? Of course there would be more children.

'It was the shock,' said Van Heerden. 'It should be next month.'

Major Carruthers leaned back against the wall of the hut and took out a cigarette clumsily. He felt weak. He felt as if Van Heerden had struck him, smiling. This was an absurd and

67

unjust feeling, but for a moment he hated Van Heerden for standing there and saying: this grey country of poverty that you fear so much, will take on a different look when you actually enter it. You will cease to exist: there is no energy left, when one is wrestling naked, with life, for your kind of fine feelings and scruples and regrets.

'We hope it will be a boy,' volunteered Van Heerden, with a tentative friendliness, as if he thought it might be considered a familiarity to offer his private emotions to Major Carruthers. 'We have five boys and four girls – three girls,' he corrected himself, his face contracting.

Major Carruthers asked stiffly: 'Will she be all right?'

'I do it,' said Van Heerden. 'The last was born in the middle of the night, when it was raining. That was when we were in the tent. It's nothing to her,' he added, with pride. He was listening, as he spoke, to the slow moaning from inside. 'I'd better be getting in to her,' he said, knocking out his pipe against the mud of the walls. Nodding to Major Carruthers, he lifted the sack and disappeared.

After a while Major Carruthers gathered himself together and forced himself to walk erect across the clearing under the curious gaze of the children. His mind was fixed and numb, but he walked as if moving to a destination. When he reached the house, he at once pulled paper and pen towards him and wrote, and each slow difficult word was a nail in the coffin of his pride as a man.

Some minutes later he went in to his wife. She was awake, turned on her side, watching the door for the relief of his coming. 'I've written for a job at Home,' he said simply, laying his hand on her thin dry wrist, and feeling the slow pulse beat up suddenly against his palm.

He watched curiously as her face crumpled and the tears of thankfulness and release ran slowly down her cheeks and soaked the pillow.

The Boss

Dan Jacobson

'AND THIS,' MR KRAMER said to Miss Posen, 'is my son, Lionel.'

'Mr Kramer! You're teasing me,' Miss Posen said reprovingly.

The old man winked at his son, who stood with him at Miss Posen's desk. Embarrassed but proud, determined not to reveal the quiver within him, Lionel turned to go to the next room, but his father took him by the sleeve. 'You must let Miss Posen have a good look, so that she'll remember you.'

'Oh, Mr Kramer!'

And the young man said: 'Miss Posen's seen me often enough.'

'But you are different now. We are all different, aren't we, Lily, now that the younger generation has come to take our place?'

The boy was smiling, flattered but a little wearied by his father's pleasure in him. 'I'm no different from what I was. And we're interfering with Miss Posen's work.'

'Do you hear that?' Mr Kramer jokingly shook his finger at Miss Posen. 'Already Lionel is worrying about the work. It's a good sign, Lily. We'll all have to work hard now that he is here. New hands and a new young man make a new order.'

It seemed that Miss Posen could respond only by shaking her head and blushing slightly. But she managed to say: 'You're young enough, Mr Kramer – ' She shook her head again.

'How can you say that, when the proof is standing here next to me that one of these days I must go?' The old man spoke mischievously, provoking them both.

'I don't believe it,' Miss Posen said, looking down at the papers on her desk.

There was a sudden pause. Frightened at the effect of her words Miss Posen said: 'All I can do is to carry on with my work. That's all you want of me, Mr Kramer?'

'Of course.'

'Come, Dad.'

'I'm coming, I'm coming.' And the old man followed his son, who was already half-way down the office. But at the door he turned and said to Miss Posen, smiling as he spoke,

'You see, already he is giving me orders.'

To Lionel Mr Kramer said, in his own office, 'Poor girl. Did you see how red she went?' Screwing up his face he scratched at his cheek several times, with the back of his nails, roughly, almost contemptuously. 'On her cheeks here,' he said 'You'd think she was still seventeen.'

'She's a long way from seventeen,' the son said, who was eighteen. He was sitting in the chair in front of the desk.

'A long way,' the father agreed. 'Poor girl!' Miss Posen was over forty, but Mr Kramer almost invariably referred to her with scorn and affection as a 'poor girl' – she was so plain and dull, and would never get married. Because he had come to South Africa as an immigrant boy and was now entirely through his own efforts the manager of a large butter factory, he could afford to be scornful of failures like Lily Posen. But he reminded his son, 'It's a long time she's been here, yet she still does a good day's work, she doesn't let up.'

'I know, I know. You talk as if I'm a stranger here. Christ, I grew up in the factory – I've always been here. What is this nonsense of yours? – introducing me to Miss Posen and all the others in the office. It just makes me look ridiculous.'

'You don't have to worry about that. You don't look ridiculous to them so easily.'

'You don't understand.'

'No –?' the father asked, his eyes moving sharply towards his son. But he restrained himself. 'And now for some tea.'

'When do I start work?'

'After tea.' Mr Kramer pressed the bell on his desk, and when a girl came in he asked, 'How about some tea, Betty? Two cups, please.'

The father was the first to speak after she had left the office. 'So you don't think you'll regret it, now that you've seen it all?'

'I've told you, Dad, I've seen it a thousand times.'

'With a difference. Now it isn't a matter of coming here for a few weeks in your school holidays, or for an afternoon when you've been to town with some friends. Now it's every day, every

morning – the same things, the same work, the same people
... You won't be jealous when your friends come from the
university and tell you what a good time they're having there?'

'I won't be jealous. We've been over all this before. I don't
want to go to the university.' Lionel's voice was querulous. He
was tall, tanned, with a lean face and large brown eyes – physically unlike his father, but with something of his father's shrugging movements in his shoulders. 'I'm not interested in wasting
my time. And your money. I'm here, I know what I'm doing.'

They waited in silence for the tea to come in. When it did
Lionel drank his quickly, put the cup back on the tray, and
stood up. 'I'm starting work now.'

'Ask Barton to show you the accounts. Your first job is to
learn some names.'

At the door Lionel turned; he pushed the door to and fro in
his hand for a moment. 'You'll see, Dad. You'll be able to
depend on me. I'm not scared of responsibility.'

'That's what I want, Lionel. I'm getting to be an old man,
and I think I'll be glad to rely on you.' Seeing the slight trim
figure of his son, standing there half-defiant and half-afraid in
his brown business suit, the old man's heart moved with pride
and pain in his breast.

Often Mr Kramer sat lazily in his office in the mornings,
drinking tea, reading the papers and the correspondence that
came in, studying – out of an unceasing curiosity and respect
for the things of this world – the advertisements for goods he
would never buy. But on Lionel's first day at work he was up
and about all day. Squat, his skull shining, his shoulders
broad, he walked about eagerly and authoritatively, one hand
flying up to acknowledge an employee's greeting: he went backwards and forwards between the office block and the factory,
at ease and in command in both. For his employees he had a
hasty paternal regard; he was easy with them, for he knew they
were dependent on him.

He went with Lionel, or he followed Lionel and spoke to those
Lionel had just spoken to, or he merely watched; and by the

end of the day he was able to say to Miss Posen, 'The boy is shaping well. Soon Lionel will really be ordering me around.'

'No, Mr Kramer.'

Curiously, humorously, Mr Kramer watched her. 'You think not, Lily?'

'No one has ever told you what to do, not as long as I've been here. And you know how long that is, Mr Kramer.'

'Everything begins, and everything ends, sooner or later.'

'No, Mr Kramer,' Miss Posen said, daring to insist. And as a reward he gave her a lift home that evening.

Before Lionel had come to work in the firm, when he had been a schoolboy, all the white employees had called him Lionel; now that he was working in a position of authority among them, they called him Mr Lionel. All but Miss Posen. She presumed on the fact that she was the oldest employee, both in age and in years of service; and she continued to call him Lionel. She presumed too – Lionel secretly was sure – on the fact that she was the only Jewish employee, and he hated the last presumption even more than he did the others, for it seemed to drag him down to a level where he was forever equal with her.

After a few weeks he complained to his father. 'No one else calls me just Lionel. Why should she? It sets a bad example to everyone else in the office.'

'Yes,' Mr Kramer agreed.

'She tries to pretend that I don't matter around here, that I'm still a little boy.'

'Then you must show her that you're not.'

Lionel had hoped that somehow his father might do that for him, but now he had no choice in the matter. A few days passed before he could bring himself to do it, but in the end he did call Miss Posen into his father's office, and in his father's presence he told her that he wanted her to call him Mr Lionel. His courage almost failed him, and he wheedled her: 'I know it's hard for you, because you've been here for so long, and can remember me when I was just a little boy, but so can others on the staff. I have that against me, and I want you to set an example to them.'

Miss Posen moved her hands, clasped in front of her bosom, uneasily within one another. She was heavily built and bespectacled; her glasses were tinged faintly blue, and she usually wore blue dresses and blue jumpers – 'to match,' Mr Kramer had once said, 'her glasses'. She had been so long in the office that she could do any work she was asked to do: typing, sending out accounts and farmers' cheques, supervising the work of the other girls, a certain amount of bookkeeping. But for all the slowness of her movements and the heaviness of her figure, the years as they passed had done nothing to wear out of her a kind of girlishness that could as easily find expression in a blush and a giggle of excitement as in a silly settled obstinacy.

Now she stood dumb in the office, blushing faintly. Her blue glasses sought for instruction from Mr Kramer's gaze. But the old man stared to one side, as if unconscious of the plea.

'I wouldn't mind you calling me whatever you like when we're alone like this,' Lionel said, wheedling again. 'But in the office, with the others there – I'd be glad of your cooperation.' The last phrase sounded so business-like he was able to bring it out briskly.

'It's difficult for me to remember,' Miss Posen said with a start. Her voice was uncertain – she was still looking for support or even response from Lionel's father. There was none; and she seemed to give in, to surrender. 'I will try, Lionel. I suppose that – that – I've been here so long. . . . I can remember when you used to come to me for sweets.'

'That's over now.'

'I suppose it is – if you want –'

'I've told you what I want.'

Lionel got to his feet, and opened the door for her, as a consolation, and she went out with a last look back, in time to see Mr Kramer pulling hard but still absently at his cheek with the thumb and forefinger of one hand.

Lionel felt virtuous, having done what he had. 'That settles that,' he said to his father.

But that had not settled that. For Miss Posen continued to call Lionel just Lionel. The first few times it happened Lionel told himself that it was merely a slip on her part. But she persisted. She called him Lionel as if she couldn't imagine calling him anything else, as if he had never spoken to her.

Eventually Lionel complained to his father again. 'She's sly. She pretends she doesn't know what she's doing, but she knows well enough. She's doing it on purpose. She wants to drag me down.'

'Why should she want to do that?'

'You know why,' Lionel said bluntly. 'It's obvious – I don't know why you pretend that you don't. She's old and finished and she's got it against me because I'm young and on top of her.'

Mr Kramer shrugged his shoulders. 'Speak to her again, if you're so cross.'

This time Lionel spoke privately to Miss Posen, less wheedlingly and more harshly; and again she promised that she would mend her ways. An hour later she called him Lionel. And not only did she continue to call him just Lionel; she became, as Lionel described it to his father, 'cheeky'. Still heavy, reluctant, hard-working, she nevertheless was cheeky as well – and cheeky publicly, cheeky in front of other members of the staff, cheeky even in front of Lionel's father. 'You'll do this for me, won't you Miss Posen?' Lionel might say, and she'd simply say, 'No'. Or he'd say, 'Get that file for me, Miss Posen,' and she, with her eyes downcast, her voice low, would answer, 'Get it yourself.'

Lionel could hardly believe his ears, when she spoke to him like this. He went pale, under his tanned skin; his dark eyes stared forward: then he would move, he would do the job himself, working brusquely, pretending to be concerned only with the business in hand. And though the others in the office were wary after each incident, once the shock had passed they wondered, Lionel was sure, what they too might one day be able to get away with.

'You've heard the way she talks to me,' Lionel said to his father. 'It's impossible, things can't go on like this. You've got to do something with her, Dad.'

'If I bring her in here, and speak to her severely, certainly she'll stop being cheeky to you. But it will be because of me, not because of you. She'll think less of you, and so will everyone else in the office when they hear of it. They will think that Mr Lionel can't look after himself, that he has to come running to his father like a little boy. Is that what you want them to think of you?'

'If you really wanted to help me, you'd find a way to do it.'

'Lionel, this is a battle, it's your first battle. You must win it by yourself, or you won't have confidence when the next one comes. And who are you fighting against, after all? Only that poor girl, Lily Posen, who sits like dough in the office. Can't you get the better of her?'

'You're on her side!' Lionel shouted suddenly.

Mr Kramer seemed undisturbed by the accusation. Smiling, his eyes half-closed, he said, 'Lionel, I am on my side. That's what I'm trying to teach you – to be for yourself.'

'All right,' Lionel warned his father, 'you'll see. I'll fix this business by myself. And then you'll know too.'

So Lionel watched Miss Posen, watching for his opportunity. No one had ever watched her before; and Lionel was rewarded when for the first time he opened her handbag in the secrecy of the lavatory and found in it a small roll of penny stamps. The stamps might have been her own, but he was sure they were not. He did not say anything about it at the time – he merely made a note of the date, and the amount of the stamps, and returned the bag to its place on her desk. Then whenever he could – when she was out on some message to the factory and there was no one else in her office – he opened her bag to see what he could find. He found a typewriter-ribbon in a still-sealed tin; he found erasers; a box of paper-clips, a rubber thimble, a ball-point pen. All of these things he put back in her bag, making a note of what each had been, and the date on which he had found it. Soon he had a little dossier on Miss Posen's pilfering; he looked back with pride to the day he had noticed that certain items of stationery were disappearing faster than they should have been from the stationery-cabinet – to which Miss Posen, as the oldest employee, had a key. And he looked forward with resolution to the day when he would confront her with what she had done.

One morning Lionel went into the office that she shared with another girl; Miss Posen was standing at the filing-cabinet, going through some papers. Lionel asked her:

'Have you got the figures I wanted yesterday?'

'No.'

'When will you have them?'

'When they're ready, Lionel.' She went on with the sorting of her papers.

'When will that be?' Lionel's voice was loud with anger.

Hers was low. 'Say the bells of Stepney.'

Lionel knew that his father would be out of the office that afternoon.

'I'll speak to you later,' he said. 'Come into my father's office at three o'clock.'

At three o'clock he was seated at his father's desk with the sheet of paper containing her record on the table in front of him. When she came in, he spoke without looking up, hardly opening his mouth, so that his voice would not tremble. 'Miss Posen, I have something very important to speak to you about.' He did not invite her to sit down. 'On the twelfth of October you took from this office penny stamps to the value of one shilling. On the seventeenth of October you took a box of paper-clips. On the eighteenth, an unused pencil. On the first of November, three pencils . . .' And so he went on, down the list. He forced himself to look up when he had finished. 'What have you got to say about that? You've been stealing from us.'

When he saw her – so old, so dull, her shoulders hanging

uselessly in her blue dress – Lionel's fear left him, and so too did his shame. He could stare hard at her, he could shout at her if he wanted to. Suddenly he knew his own power, and he was enraged. 'You're a thief! My father has employed you for fifteen years, and you repay everything he's done for you by stealing from him! What are you without him? Nothing! Nothing! And you steal from him!'

Miss Posen did not burst into tears, as he was expecting her to. She turned and almost ran out of the office. The heavy, fugitive, graceless scuttle fed his rage with her again.

When his father came back from town he told him what had happened. 'She's got to go,' Lionel shouted. 'I've found her out and she's got to go. I've shown who I am now!' He was pale, his hand was trembling, but his eyes were bright, and Mr Kramer could see that he had tasted blood, that he was exulting in his own power.

Between his son and Miss Posen, Mr Kramer did not have a moment's hesitation as to which he should choose. One of the two had to go now, and it would not be his son. But it was for his own position too that the old man knew he had to fight.

So he listened to Lionel, and when Lionel had exhausted himself and had slumped suddenly into a chair, Mr Kramer said quietly, 'Now I want to speak to Miss Posen.' When Lionel sat where he was Mr Kramer said, 'I want to speak to her alone. I want to find out the truth of what has been happening.'

'The truth! What do you mean?'

Mr Kramer ignored the protest. 'Tell Miss Posen that I want to see her, and then go and make yourself busy somewhere.'

Miss Posen broke down when Mr Kramer said gently to her, 'It was a foolish thing for you to do, Lily.' Miss Posen wept; the tears stole down under her blue glasses, and she lifted them to wipe the tears away, showing Mr Kramer a glimpse of two large, wet, naked eyes. But even before she had finished drying her eyes, Mr Kramer had haltingly begun to explain why he could not give her another chance.

'I would, Lily,' he said. 'You've been working for me for fifteen years, and that means something to me. But I can't.'

'Please, Mr Kramer – please help me. I don't know why I've been taking these things – I haven't been doing it for long –.'

'I know. Ever since Lionel's been here.'

Miss Posen was silenced; she stood stiff, as if shocked at what he had said. Seeing this Mr Kramer explained; 'I know how long you've been doing it, not because I've been watching you, Lily, but because I know how these things are. Shouldn't I know? Shouldn't I know better than anyone else in the world how you are feeling? Am I not in the same position? And that's why I can't give you another chance, Lily. It's that boy, that Lionel. You see how fierce he is. He's a youngster, but I can't go against him. I'm not strong enough. I'm telling you this, Lily, because you've been with me for fifteen years – to anyone else I wouldn't tell such a thing, I'd be too ashamed.' He spoke so haltingly and with such small shrugs of his shoulders, with such a downcast head, that Miss Posen almost tried to comfort him. But he would not accept her comfort. 'It's what I told you the first day he was here,' he said. 'My time is finished.'

Later he promised her that he would see to it that she got another position with some other firm in town, just as good a position as the one she was leaving. 'I know it will not be the same,' he said, 'but it is the best that I can do, with that boy here. And I will do it. We'll say that you're leaving because you and Lionel couldn't get on well together, and that's the only reason. Lionel will keep his mouth closed, he's the kind of strong boy who can.'

When she left the office, Miss Posen passed Lionel in the corridor outside. As a result of Mr Kramer's words she had recovered sufficiently to say fiercely to him, 'You're a dirty little boy!' Suddenly bright red and pale blue she exclaimed, 'You should be ashamed of yourself!'

Lionel came sideways into his father's office, looking back. 'You hear what she said?' He was amazed that she should have turned on him.

'Yes, I heard,' Mr Kramer said, with no expression in his voice. 'I've done it,' he told Lionel. 'You can be happy now. She's going, I've told her to get out, poor girl, and she won't be worrying you any longer.'

'It isn't just that she was worrying me! She was stealing!'

'Miss Posen! If I had known she was taking such things, such rubbish, like pencils and stamps, after fifteen years of work, I would have turned my head away. I could never have done what you did – watching, planning, setting traps, looking into the poor girl's handbag. Miss Posen's! I would have been ashamed. And then dragging the poor girl into the office and having such a scene with her. . . .'

'Wasn't I right?' Lionel demanded. 'Didn't I find out about her?'

'By your lights, perhaps, you were right. Your lights seem to be different from mine, that's all. I'm just a man who wants peace and kindness, and who thinks that a woman has worked fifteen years . . . fifteen years! It is nearly as long as you have been alive.'

'But –'

'But you did what you thought was right. I know. I can see that. And perhaps you were right, but it isn't my way of being right. And now I've got the problem of finding a place for her just as good as the one she held here. It's the very least I can do for the poor girl, after what has happened here. Fifteen years! It's her lifetime that's passed here, and what have you given her to show for it? Ach,' the old man said, 'it's no good to think of it.'

Mr Kramer was as good as his word in getting Miss Posen a new position. He also bought her an expensive farewell present, and gave her a small party on her last afternoon in the office. At the party Lionel heard Miss Posen describe Mr Kramer as the best man she had ever known. Lionel did not know what was happening to him.

His father did nothing to enlighten him. When Lionel wanted to talk of it, all he heard from his father was, 'You did what you thought was right. Poor Miss Posen! Poor girl! And her father a little tailor! But perhaps a hard heart is a good thing to have in business nowadays, though I managed without one.'

'I haven't a hard heart,' Lionel pleaded with his father. 'Dad, I did what I thought was *right*.'

'You did it, and that was enough. Now it's over and done with and forgotten. Except by that poor Miss Posen. She'll remember, it will be like a scar on her heart, all her life.'

'Please, Dad, listen to me – '

'Who doesn't listen to you now?' Mr Kramer asked, his arms wide open, his face lifted in surprise.

'You don't,' Lionel said.

'What? Didn't I throw that poor girl out after fifteen years, push her out like she was nothing to me, because you told me to?'

'You did, I know. Oh,' Lionel said miserably, 'I don't know.'

'What don't you know?'

It was hard for Lionel to make the admission. 'Anything at all.'

Mr Kramer knew he had won his fight. 'You'll learn,' he said.

The tenderness in his voice made Lionel wonder, but to that too he had to submit.

Raspberry Jam

Angus Wilson

'HOW ARE YOUR funny friends at Potter's Farm, Johnnie?' asked his aunt from London.

'Very well, thank you, Aunt Eva,' said the little boy in the window in a high prim voice. He had been drawing faces on his bare knee and now put down the indelible pencil. The moment that he had been dreading all day had arrived. Now they would probe and probe with their silly questions and the whole story of that dreadful tea party with his old friends would come tumbling out. There would be scenes and abuse and the old ladies would be made to suffer further. This he could not bear, for although he never wanted to see them again and had come, in brooding over the afternoon's events, almost to hate them, to bring them further misery, to be the means of their disgrace would be worse than any of the horrible things that had already happened. Apart from his fear of what might follow he did not intend to pursue the conversation himself, for he disliked his aunt's bright patronizing tone. He knew that she felt ill at ease with children and would soon lapse into that embarrassing 'leg pulling' manner which some grown ups used. For himself, he did not mind this but if she made silly jokes about the old ladies at Potter's Farm he would get angry and then Mummy would say all that about his having to learn to take a joke and about his being highly strung and where could he have got it from, not from her.

But he need not have feared. For though the grown ups continued to speak of the old ladies as 'Johnnie's friends', the topic soon became a general one. Many of the things the others said made the little boy bite his lip, but he was able to go on drawing on his knee with the feigned abstraction of a child among adults.

'My dear,' said Johnnie's mother to her sister, 'you really must meet them. They're the *most* wonderful pair of freaks. They live in a great barn of a farmhouse. The inside's like a museum, full of old junk mixed up with some really lovely things all mouldering to pieces. The family's been there for hundreds of years and they're madly proud of it. They won't let anyone do a single thing for them, although they're both well over sixty, and of course the result is that the place is in the most *frightful* mess. It's really rather ghastly and one oughtn't to laugh, but if you could *see* them, my dear. The elder one, Marian, wears a long tweed skirt almost to the ankles, she had a terrible hunting accident or something, and a school blazer. The younger one's said to have been a beauty, but she's really rather sinister now, inches thick in enamel and rouge and dressed in all colours of the rainbow, with dyed red hair which is constantly falling down. Of course, Johnnie's made tremendous friends with them and I must say they've been immensely kind to him, but what Harry will say when he comes back from Germany, I can't think. As it *is*, he's always complaining that the child is too much with women and has no friends of his own age.'

'I don't honestly think you need worry about that, Grace,' said her brother Jim, assuming the attitude of the sole male in the company, for of the masculinity of old Mr Codrington their guest he instinctively made little. 'Harry ought to be very pleased with the way old Miss Marian's encouraged Johnnie's cricket and riding; it's pretty uphill work, too. Johnnie's not exactly a Don Bradman or a Gordon Richards, are you, old man? I like the old girl, personally. She's got a bee in her bonnet about the Bolsheviks, but she's stood up to those damned council people about the drainage like a good 'un; she does no end for the village people as well and says very little about it.'

'I don't like the sound of "doing good to the village" very much,' said Eva, 'it usually means patronage and disappointed old maids meddling in other people's affairs. It's only in villages like this that people can go on serving out sermons with gifts of soup.'

'Curiously enough, Eva old dear,' Jim said, for he believed in being rude to his progressive sister, 'in this particular case you happen to be wrong. Miss Swindale is extremely broad-minded. You remember, Grace,' he said, addressing his other sister, 'what she said about giving money to old Cooper, when the rector protested it would only go on drink – "You have a perfect right to consign us all to hell, rector, but you must allow us the choice of how we get there." Serve him damn well right for interfering too.'

'Well, Jim darling,' said Grace. 'I must say she could hardly have the nerve to object to drink – the poor old thing has the most dreadful bouts herself. Sometimes when I can't get gin from the grocer's it makes me absolutely livid to think of all that secret drinking and they say it only makes her more and more gloomy. All the same I suppose *I* should drink if I had a sister like Dolly. It must be horrifying when one's family-proud like she is to have such a skeleton in the cupboard. I'm sure there's going to be the most awful trouble in the village about Dolly before she's finished. You've heard the squalid story about young Tony Calkett, haven't you? My dear, he went round there to fix the lights and apparently Dolly invited him up to her bedroom to have a cherry brandy of all things and made the *most* unfortunate proposals. Of course I know she's been very lonely and it's all a ghastly tragedy really, but Mrs Calkett's a terrible silly little woman and a very jealous mother and she won't see it that way at all. The awful thing is that both the Miss Swindales give me the creeps rather. I have a dreadful feeling when I'm with them that I don't know who's the keeper and who's the lunatic. In fact, Eva my dear, they're both really rather horrors and I suppose I ought never to let Johnnie go near them.'

'I think you have no cause for alarm, Mrs Allingham,' put in old Mr Codrington in a purring voice. He had been waiting for some time to take the floor, and now that he had got it he did not intend to relinquish it. Had it not been for the small range of village society he would not have been a visitor at Mrs Allingham's, for, as he frequently remarked, if there was one thing he deplored more than her vulgarity it was her loquacity. 'No one delights in scandal more than I do, but it is always a little distorted, a trifle *exagéré*, indeed where would be its charm, if it were not so! No doubt Miss Marian has her solaces, but she remains a noble-hearted woman. No doubt Miss Dolly is often a trifle naughty' – he dwelt on this word caressingly – 'but she really only uses the privilege for one, who has been that rare thing, a beautiful woman. As for Tony Calkett it is really time that that young man ceased to be so unnecessarily virginal. If my calculations are correct, and I have every reason to think they are, he must be twenty-two, an age at which modesty should have been put behind one long since. No, dear Mrs Allingham, you should rejoice that Johnnie has been given the friendship of two women who can still, in this vulgar age, be honoured with a name that, for all that it has been cheapened and degraded, one is still proud to bestow – the name of a lady.' Mr Codrington threw his head back and stared round the room as though defying anyone to deny him his own right to this name. 'Miss Marian will encourage him in the manlier virtues, Miss Dolly in the arts. Her own water colours, though perhaps lacking in strength, are not to be despised. She has a fine sense of colour, though I could wish that she was a little less bold with it in her costume. Nevertheless with that red-gold hair there is something splendid about her appearance, something especially wistful to an old man like myself. Those peacock blue linen gowns take me back through Conder's fans and Whistler's rooms to Rossetti's Mona Vanna. Unfortunately as she gets older the linen is not overclean. We are given a Mona Vanna with the collected dust of age, but surely,' he added with a little cackle, 'it is dirt that lends patina to a picture. It is interesting that you should say you are uncertain which of the two sisters is a trifle peculiar, because, in point of fact, both have been away, as they used to phrase it in the servants' hall of my youth. Strange,' he mused, 'that one's knowledge of the servants' hall should always belong to the period of one's infancy, be, as it were, eternally outmoded. I have no conception of how they may speak of an asylum in the servants' hall of today. No doubt Johnnie could tell us. But, of course, I forget that social progress has removed the servants' hall from the ken of all but the most privileged. I wonder now whether that is a loss or a blessing in disguise.'

'A blessing without any doubt at all,' said Aunt Eva, irrepressible in the cause of Advance. 'Think of all the appalling inhibitions we acquired from servants' chatter. I had an old nurse who was always talking about ghosts and dead bodies and curses on the family in a way that must have set up terrible phobias in me. I still have those ugly, morbid nightmares about spiders,' she said, turning to Grace.

'I refuse,' said Mr Codrington in a voice of great contempt, for he was greatly displeased at the interruption, 'to believe that any dream of yours could be ugly; morbid, perhaps, but with a sense of drama and artistry that would befit the dreamer. I confess that if I have inhibitions, and I trust I have many, I cling to them. I should not wish to give way unreservedly to what is so unattractively called the libido, it suggests a state of affairs in which beach pyjamas are worn and jitterbugging is compulsory. No, let us retain the fantasies, the imaginative games of childhood, even at the expense of a little fear, for they are the true magnificence of the springtime of life.'

'Darling Mr Codrington,' cried Grace. 'I do pray and hope you're right. It's exactly what I keep on telling myself about Johnnie, but I really don't know. Johnnie, darling, run upstairs and fetch mummy's bag.' But his mother need not have been so solicitous about Johnnie's overhearing what she had to say, for the child had already left the room. 'There you are, Eva,' she said, 'he's the strangest child. He slips away without so much as a word. I must say he's very good at amusing himself, but I very much wonder if all the funny games he plays aren't very bad for him. He's certainly been very peculiar lately, strange silences and sudden tears, and, my dear, the awful nightmares he has! About a fortnight ago, after he'd been at tea with the Miss Swindales, I don't know whether it was something he'd eaten there, but he made the most awful sobbing noise in the night. Sometimes I think it's just temper, like Harry. The other day at tea I only offered him some jam, my best home-made raspberry too, and he just screamed me.'

'You should take him to a child psychologist,' said her sister.

'Well, darling, I expect you're right. It's so difficult to know whether they're frauds, everyone recommends somebody different. I'm sure Harry would disapprove too, and then think of the expense . . . You know how desperately poor we are, although I think I manage as well as anyone could.' . . . At this point Mr Codrington took a deep breath and sat back, for on the merits of her household management Grace Allingham was at her most boring and could by no possible stratagem be restrained.

Upstairs, in the room which had been known as the nursery until his eleventh birthday, but was now called his bedroom, Johnnie was playing with his farm animals. The ritual involved in the game was very complicated and had a long history. It was on his ninth birthday that he had been given the farm set by his father. 'Something a bit less babyish than those woolly animals of yours,' he had said, and Johnnie had accepted them, since they made in fact no difference whatever to the games he played; games at which could Major Allingham have guessed he would have been distinctly puzzled. The little ducks, pigs, and cows of lead no more remained themselves in Johnnie's games than had the pink woollen sheep and green cloth horses of his early childhood. Johnnie's world was a strange compound of the adult world in which he had always lived and a book world composed from Grimm, the Arabian Nights, Alice's adventures, natural history books, and more recently the novels of Dickens and Jane Austen. His imagination was taken by anything odd – strange faces, strange names, strange animals, strange voices and catchphrases – all these appeared in his games. The black pig and the white duck were keeping a hotel; the black pig was called that funny name of Granny's friend – Mrs Gudgeon-Rogers. She was always holding her skirt tight round the knees and warming her bottom over the fire – like Mrs Coates, and whenever anyone in the hotel asked for anything she would reply 'Darling, I can't stop now. I've simply got to fly,' like Aunt Sophie, and then she would fly out of the window. The duck was an Echidna, or Spiny Anteater who wore a picture hat and a fish train like in the picture of Aunt Eleanor, she used to weep a lot, because, like Granny, when she described her games of bridge, she was 'vulnerable' and she would yawn at the hotel guests and say 'Lord I am tired' like Lydia Bennet. The two collie dogs had 'been asked to leave', like in the story of Mummy's friend Gertie who 'got tight' at the Hunt Ball, they were going to be divorced and were consequently wearing 'co-respondent shoes'. The lady collie who was called Minnie Mongelheim kept on saying 'That chap's got a proud stomach. Let him eat chaff' – like Mr F's Aunt in *Little Dorrit*. The sheep, who always played the part of a bore, kept on talking like Daddy about 'leg cuts and fine shots to cover'; sometimes when the rest of the animal guests got too bored the sheep would change into Grandfather Graham and tell a funny story about a Scotsman so that they were bored in a different way. Finally the cat who was a grand vizier and worked by magic would say 'All the ways round here belong to me' like the Red Queen and he would have all the guests torn in pieces and flayed alive until Johnnie felt so sorry for them that the game could come to an end. Mummy was already saying that he was getting too old for the farm animals: one always seemed to be getting too old for something. In fact the animals were no longer necessary to Johnnie's games, for most of the time now he liked to read and when he wanted to play games he could do so in his head without the aid of any toys, but he hated the idea of throwing things away because they were no longer needed. Mummy and Daddy were always throwing things away and never thinking of their feelings. When he had been much younger Mummy had given him an old petticoat to put in the dustbin, but Johnnie had taken it to his room and hugged it and cried over it, because it was no longer wanted. Daddy had been very upset. Daddy was always being upset at what Johnnie did. Only the last time that he was home there had been an awful row, because Johnnie had tried to make up like old Mrs Langdon and could not wash the blue paint off his eyes. Daddy had beaten him and looked very hurt all day and said to Mummy that he'd 'rather see him dead than grow up a cissie'. No it was better not to do imitations oneself, but to leave it to the animals.

This afternoon, however, Johnnie was not attending seriously to his game, he was sitting and thinking of what the grown ups had been saying and of how he would never see his friends, the old ladies, again, and of how he never, never wanted to. This irrevocable separation lay like a black cloud over his mind, a constant darkness which was lit up momentarily by forks of hysterical horror, as he remembered the nature of their last meeting.

The loss of his friendship was a very serious one to the little boy. It had met so completely the needs and loneliness which are always great in a child isolated from other children and surrounded by unimaginative adults. In a totally unself-conscious way, half-crazy as they were and half-crazy even though the child sensed them to be, the Misses Swindale possessed just those qualities of which Johnnie felt most in need. To begin with they were odd and fantastic and highly coloured, and more important still they believed that such peculiarities were nothing to be ashamed of, indeed were often a matter for pride. 'How delightfully odd,' Miss Dolly would say in her drawling voice, when Johnnie told her how the duck-billed platypus had chosen spangled tights when Queen Alexandra had ordered her to be shot from a cannon at Brighton Pavilion. 'What a delightfully extravagant creature that duck-billed platypus is, Caro Gabricle,' for Miss Dolly had brought back a touch of Italian here and there from her years in Florence, whilst in Johnnie she fancied a likeness to the angel Gabriel. In describing her own dresses, too, which she would do for hours on end, extravagance was her chief commendation, 'as for that gold and silver brocade ball dress' she would say and her voice would sink to an awed whisper 'it was richly fantastic'. To Miss Marian, with her more brusque, masculine nature, Johnnie's imaginative powers were a matter of far greater wonder than to her sister and she treated them with even greater respect. In her bluff, simple way like some old-fashioned religious army officer or overgrown but solemn schoolboy, she too admired the eccentric and unusual. 'What a lark!' she would say, when Johnnie told her how the Crown Prince had slipped in some polar bears dressed in pink ballet skirts to sing 'Ta Ra Ra boomdeay' in the middle of a boring school concert which his royal duties had forced him to attend. 'What a nice chap he must be to know.' In talking of her late father, the general, whose memory she worshipped and of whom she had a never ending flow of anecdotes, she would give an instance of his warmhearted but distinctly eccentric behaviour and say in her gruff voice 'Wasn't it rum? That's the bit I like best.' But in neither of the sisters was there the least trace of that self-conscious whimsicality which Johnnie had met and hated in so many grown ups. They were the first people he had met who liked what he liked and as he liked it.

Their love of lost causes and their defence of the broken, the worn out, and the forgotten met a deep demand in his nature, which had grown almost sickly sentimental in the dead practical world of his home. He loved the disorder of the old eighteenth-century farm house, the collection of miscellaneous objects of all kinds that littered the rooms, and thoroughly sympathized with the sisters' magpie propensity to collect dress ends, feathers, string, old whistles, and broken cups. He grew excited with them in their fights to prevent drunken old men being taken to workhouses and cancerous old women to hospitals, though he sensed something crazy in their constant fear of intruders, bolsheviks, and prying doctors. He would often try to change the conversation when Miss Marian became excited about spies in the village, or told him of how torches had been flashing all night in the garden and of how the vicar was slandering her father's memory in a whispering campaign. He felt deeply embarrassed when Miss Dolly insisted on looking into all the cupboards and behind the curtains to see, as she said 'if there were any eyes or ears where they were not wanted. For,

Caro Gabriele, those who hate beauty are many and strong, those who love it are few.'

It was, above all, their kindness and their deep affection which held the love-starved child. His friendship with Miss Dolly had been almost instantaneous. She soon entered into his fantasies with complete intimacy, and he was spellbound by her stories of the gaiety and beauty of Mediterranean life. They would play dressing up games together and enacted all his favourite historical scenes. She helped him with his French too, and taught him Italian words with lovely sounds; she praised his painting and helped him to make costume designs for some of his 'characters'. With Miss Marian, at first, there had been much greater difficulty. She was an intensely shy woman and took refuge behind a rather forbidding bluntness of manner. Her old-fashioned military airs and general 'manly' tone, copied from her father, with which she approached small boys, reminded Johnnie too closely of his own father. 'Head up, me lad,' she would say, 'shoulders straight.' Once he had come very near to hating her, when after an exhibition of his absentmind-edness she had said 'Take care, Johnnie head in the air. You'll be lost in the clouds, me lad, if you're not careful.' But the moment after she had won his heart for ever, when with a little chuckle she continued 'Jolly good thing if you are, you'll learn things up there that we shall never know.' On her side, as soon as she saw that she had won his affection, she lost her shyness and proceeded impulsively to load him with kindness. She loved to cook his favourite dishes for him and give him his favourite fruit from their kitchen garden. Her admiration for his precocity and imagination was open-eyed and childlike. Finally they had found a common love of Dickens and Jane Austen, which she had read with her father, and now they would sit for hours talking over the characters in their favourite books.

Johnnie's affection for them was intensely protective, and increased daily as he heard and saw the contempt and dislike with which they were regarded by many persons in the village. The knowledge that 'they had been away' was nothing new to him when Mr Codrington had revealed it that afternoon. Once Miss Dolly had told him how a foolish doctor had advised her to go into a home 'for you know, caro, ever since I returned to these grey skies my health has not been very good. People here think me strange, I cannot attune myself to the cold northern soul. But it was useless to keep me there, I need beauty and warmth of colour, and there it was so drab. The people, too, were unhappy crazy creatures and I missed my music so dreadfully.' Miss Marian had spoken more violently of it on one of her 'funny' days, when from the depredations caused by the village boys to the orchard she had passed on to the strange man she had found spying in her father's library and the need for a high wall round the house to prevent people peering through the telescopes from Mr Hatton's house opposite. 'They're frightened of us, though, Johnnie,' she had said, 'I'm too honest for them and Dolly's too clever. They're always trying to separate us. Once they took me away against my will. They couldn't keep me, I wrote to all sorts of big pots, friends of Father's, you know, and they had to release me.' Johnnie realized, too, that when his mother had said that she never knew which was the keeper, she had spoken more truly than she understood. Each sister was constantly alarmed for the other and anxious to hide the other's defects from an un-understanding world. Once when Miss Dolly had been telling him a long story about a young waiter who had slipped a note into her hand the last time she had been in London, Miss Marian called Johnnie into the kitchen to look at some pies she had made. Later she had told him not to listen if Dolly said 'soppy things' because being so beautiful she did not realize that she was no longer young. Another day when Miss Marian had brought in the silver-framed photo of her father in full dress uniform and had asked Johnnie to swear an oath to clear the general's memory in the village, Miss Dolly had begun to play a mazurka on the piano. Later, she too had warned Johnnie not to take too much notice when her sister got excited. 'She lives a little too much in the past, Gabriele. She suffered very much when our father died. Poor Marian, it is a pity perhaps that she is so good, she has had too little of the pleasures of life. But we must love her very much, caro, very much.'

Johnnie had sworn to himself to stand by them and to fight the wicked people who said they were old and useless and in the way. But now, since that dreadful tea-party, he could not fight for them any longer, for he knew why they had been shut up and felt that it was justified. In a sense, too, he understood that it was to protect others that they had to be restrained, for the most awful memory of all that terrifying afternoon was the thought that he had shared with pleasure for a moment in their wicked game.

It was certainly most unfortunate that Johnnie should have been invited to tea on that Thursday, for the Misses Swindale had been drinking heavily on and off for the preceding week, and were by that time in a state of mental and nervous excitement that rendered them far from normal. A number of events had combined to produce the greatest sense of isolation in these old women whose sanity in any event hung by a precarious thread. Miss Marian had been involved in an unpleasant scene with the vicar over the new hall for the Young People's Club. She was, as usual, providing the cash for the building and felt extremely happy and excited at being consulted about the decorations. Though she did not care for the vicar, she set out to see him, determined that she would accommodate herself to changing times. In any case, since she was the benefactress, it was, she felt, particularly necessary that she should take a back seat, to have imposed her wishes in any way would have been most ill-bred. It was an unhappy chance that caused the vicar to harp upon the need for new fabrics for the chairs and even to digress upon the ugliness of the old upholstery, for these chairs had come from the late General Swindale's library. Miss Marian was immediately reminded of her belief that the vicar was attempting secretly to blacken her father's memory, nor was the impression corrected when he tactlessly suggested that the question of her father's taste was unimportant and irrelevant. She was more deeply wounded still to find in the next few days that the village shared the vicar's view that she was attempting to dictate to the boys' club by means of her money. 'After all,' as Mrs Grove at the Post Office said, 'it's not only the large sums that count, Miss Swindale, it's all the boys' sixpences that they've saved up.' 'You've too much of your father's ways in you, that's the trouble, Miss Swindale,' said Mr Norton, who was famous for his bluntness, 'and they won't do nowadays.'

She had returned from this unfortunate morning's shopping to find Mrs Calkett on the doorstep. Now the visit of Mrs Calkett was not altogether unexpected, for Miss Marian had guessed from chance remarks of her sister's that something 'unfortunate' had happened with young Tony. When, however, the sharp-faced unpleasant little woman began to complain about Miss Dolly with innuendos and veiledly coarse suggestions, Miss Marian could stand it no longer and drove her away harshly. 'How dare you speak about my sister in that disgusting way, you evil-minded woman,' she said. 'You'd better be careful or you'll find yourself charged with libel.' When the scene was over, she felt very tired. It was dreadful of course that anyone so mean and cheap should speak thus of anyone so fine and beautiful as Dolly, but it was also dreadful that Dolly should have made such a scene possible.

Things were not improved, therefore, when Dolly returned from Brighton at once elevated by a new conquest and depressed by its subsequent results. It seemed that the new conductor on the Southdown 'that charming dark Italian-looking boy I was telling you about, my dear' had returned her a most intimate smile and pressed her hand when giving her change. Her own smiles must have been embarrassingly intimate, for a woman in the next seat had remarked loudly to her friend, 'These painted old things. Really, I wonder the men don't smack their faces.' 'I couldn't help smiling,' remarked Miss Dolly, 'she was so evidently *jalouse*, my dear. I'm glad to say the conductor did not hear, for no doubt he would have felt it necessary to come to my defence, he was so completely *épris*.'

But, for once, Miss Marian was too vexed to play ball, she turned on her sister and roundly condemned her conduct, ending up by accusing her of bringing misery to them both and shame to their father's memory. Poor Miss Dolly just stared in bewilderment, her baby blue eyes round with fright, tears washing the mascara from her eyelashes in black streams down the wrinkled vermilion of her cheeks. Finally she ran crying up to her room.

That night both the sisters began to drink heavily. Miss Dolly lay like some monstrous broken doll, her red hair streaming over her shoulders, her corsets unloosed and her fat body poking out of an old pink velvet ball dress – pink with red hair was always so audacious – through the most unexpected places in bulges of thick blue-white flesh. She sipped at glass after glass of gin, sometimes staring into the distance with bewilderment that she should find herself in such a condition, sometimes leering pruriently at some pictures of Johnny Weismuller in swimsuits that she had cut out of *Film Weekly*. At last she began to weep to think that she had sunk to this. Miss Marian sat at her desk and drank more deliberately from a cut glass decanter of brandy. She read solemnly through her father's letters, their old-fashioned, earnest Victorian sentiments swimming ever more wildly before her eyes. But, at last, she, too, began to weep as she thought of how his memory would be quite gone when she passed away, and of how she had broken the promise that she had made to him on his deathbed to stick to her sister through thick and thin.

So they continued for two or three days with wild spasms of drinking and horrible, sober periods of remorse. They cooked themselves odd scraps in the kitchen, littering the house with unwashed dishes and cups, but never speaking, always avoiding each other. They didn't change their clothes or wash, and indeed made little alteration in their appearance. Miss Dolly put fresh rouge on her cheeks periodically and some pink roses in her hair which hung there wilting; she was twice sick over the pink velvet dress. Miss Marian put on an old scarlet hunting waistcoat of her father's, partly out of maudlin sentiment and partly because she was cold. Once she fell on the stairs and cut her forehead against the banisters; the red and white handkerchief which she tied round her head gave her the appearance of a tipsy pirate. On the fourth day, the sisters were reconciled and sat in Miss Dolly's room. That night they slept, lying heavily against each other on Miss Dolly's bed, open-mouthed and snoring, Miss Marian's deep guttural rattle contrasting with Miss Dolly's high-pitched whistle. They awoke on Thursday morning, much sobered, to the realization that Johnnie was coming to tea that afternoon.

It was characteristic that neither spoke a word of the late debauch. Together they went out into the hot July sunshine to gather raspberries for Johnnie's tea. But the nets in the kitchen garden had been disarranged and the birds had got the fruit. The awful malignity of this chance event took some time to pierce through the fuddled brains of the two ladies, as they stood there grotesque and obscene in their staring pink and clashing red, with their heavy pouchy faces and bloodshot eyes showing up in the hard, clear light of the sun. But when the realization did get home it seemed to come as a confirmation of all the beliefs of persecution which had been growing throughout the drunken orgy. There is little doubt that they were both a good deal mad when they returned to the house.

Johnnie arrived punctually at four o'clock, for he was a small boy of exceptional politeness. Miss Marian opened the door to him, and he was surprised at her appearance in her red bandana and her scarlet waistcoat, and especially by her voice which, though friendly and gruff as usual, sounded thick and flat. Miss Dolly, too, looked more than usually odd with one eye closed in a kind of perpetual wink, and with her pink dress falling off her shoulders. She kept on laughing in a silly, high giggle. The shock of discovering that the raspberries were gone had driven them back to the bottle and they were both fairly drunk. They pressed upon the little boy, who was thirsty after his walk, two small glasses in succession, one of brandy, the other of gin, though in their sober mood the ladies would have died rather than have seen their little friend take strong liquor. The drink soon combined with the heat of the day and the smell of vomit that hung around the room to make Johnnie feel most strange. The walls of the room seemed to be closing in and the floor to be moving up and down like sea waves. The ladies' faces came up at him suddenly and then receded, now Miss Dolly's with great blobs of blue and scarlet and her eyes winking and leering, now Miss Marian's a huge white mass with her moustache grown large and black. He was only conscious by fits and starts of what they were doing or saying. Sometimes he would hear Miss Marian speaking in a flat, slow monotone. She seemed to be reading out her father's letters, snatches of which came to him clearly and then faded away. 'There is so much to be done in our short sojourn on this earth, so much that may be done for good, so much for evil. Let us earnestly endeavour to keep the good steadfastly before us,' then suddenly 'Major Campbell has told me of his decision to leave the regiment. I pray God hourly that he may have acted in full consideration of the Higher Will to which . . .,' and once grotesquely, 'Your Aunt Maud was here yesterday, she is a maddening woman and I consider it a just judgement upon the Liberal party that she should espouse its cause.' None of these phrases meant anything to the little boy, but he was dimly conscious that Miss Marian was growing excited, for he heard her say 'That was our father. As Shakespeare says "He was a man take him all in all" Johnnie. We loved him, but there were those who sought to destroy him, for he was too big for them. But their day is nearly ended. Always remember that, Johnnie.' It was difficult to hear all that the elder sister said, for Miss Dolly kept on drawling and giggling in his ear about a black charmeuse evening gown she had worn, and a young donkeyboy she had danced with in the fiesta at Asti. *'E come era bello, caro Gabriele, come era bello*. And afterwards . . . but I must spare the ears of one so young the details of the *arte dell' amore*,' she added with a giggle and then with drunken dignity, 'it would not be immodest I think to mention that his skin was like velvet. Only a few lire, too, just imagine.' All this, too, was largely meaningless to the boy, though he remembered it in later years.

For a while he must have slept, since he remembered that later he could see and hear more clearly though his head ached terribly. Miss Dolly was seated at the piano playing a little jig and bobbing up and down like a mountainous pink blancmange, whilst Miss Marian more than ever like a pirate was dancing some sort of a hornpipe. Suddenly Miss Dolly stopped playing. 'Shall we show him the prisoner?' she said solemnly. 'Head up, shoulders straight,' said Miss Marian in a parody of her old manner, 'you're going to be very honoured, me lad. Promise you'll never betray that honour. You shall see one of the enemy punished. Our father gave us close instructions. "Do good to all" he said "but if you catch one of the enemy, remember you are a solder's daughters." We shall obey that command.' Meanwhile Miss Dolly had returned from the kitchen, carrying a little bird which was pecking and clawing at the net in which it had been caught and shrilling incessantly – it was a little bullfinch. 'You're a very beautiful little bird,' Miss Dolly whispered, 'with lovely soft pink feathers and pretty grey wings. But you're a very naughty little bird too, *tanto cattivo*. You came and took the fruit from us which we'd kept for our darling Gabriele.' She began feverishly to pull the rose breast feathers from the bird, which piped more loudly and squirmed. Soon little trickles of red blood ran down among the feathers. 'Scarlet and pink a very daring combination,' Miss Dolly cried. Johnnie watched from his chair, his heart beating fast. Suddenly Miss Marian stepped forward and holding the bird's head she thrust a pin into his eyes. 'We don't like spies around here looking at what we are doing,' she said in her flat, gruff voice. 'When we find them we teach them a lesson so that they don't spy on us again.' Then she took out a little pocket knife and cut into the bird's breast; its wings were beating more feebly now and it claws only moved spasmodically, whilst its chirping was very faint. Little yellow and white strings of entrails began to peep out from where she had cut. 'Oh!' cried Miss Dolly, 'I like the lovely colours, I don't like these worms.' But Johnnie could bear it no longer, white and shaking he jumped from his chair and seizing the bird he threw it on the floor and then he stamped on it violently until it was nothing but a sodden crimson mass. 'Oh, Gabriele, what have you done? You've spoilt all the soft, pretty colours. Why it's nothing now, it looks just looks like a lump of raspberry jam. Why have you done it, Gabriele?' cried Miss Dolly. But little Johnnie gave no answer, he had run from the room.

The Saint

V. S. Pritchett

WHEN I WAS seventeen years old I lost my religious faith. It had been unsteady for some time and then, very suddenly, it went as the result of an incident in a punt on the river outside the town where we lived. My uncle, with whom I was obliged to stay for long periods of my life, had started a small furniture-making business in the town. He was always in difficulties about money, but he was convinced that in some way God would help him. And this happened. An investor arrived who belonged to a sect called the Church of the Last Purification, of Toronto, Canada. Could we imagine, this man asked, a good and omnipotent God allowing His children to be short of money? We had to admit we could not imagine this. The man paid some capital into my uncle's business and we were converted. Our family were the first Purifiers – as they were called – in the town. Soon a congregation of fifty or more were meeting every Sunday in a room at the Corn Exchange.

At once we found ourselves isolated and hated people. Everyone made jokes about us. We had to stand together because we were sometimes dragged into the courts. What the unconverted could not forgive in us was first that we believed in successful prayer and, secondly, that our revelation came from Toronto. The success of our prayers had a simple foundation. We regarded it as 'Error' – our name for Evil – to believe the evidence of our senses, and if we had influenza or consumption, or had lost our money or were unemployed, we denied the reality of these things, saying that since God could not have made them they therefore did not exist. It was exhilarating to look at our congregation and to know that what the vulgar would call miracles were performed among us, almost as a matter of routine, every day. Not very big miracles, perhaps, but up in London and out in Toronto, we knew that deafness and blindness, cancer and insanity, the great scourges, were constantly vanishing before the prayers of the more advanced Purifiers.

'What!' said my schoolmaster, an Irishman with eyes like broken glass and a sniff of irritability in the bristles of his nose.

'What! Do you have the impudence to tell me that if you fell off the top floor of this building and smashed your head in, you would say you hadn't fallen and were not injured?'

I was a small boy and very afraid of everybody, but not when it was a question of my religion. I was used to the kind of conundrum the Irishman had set. It was useless to argue, though our religion had already developed an interesting casuistry.

'I *would* say so,' I replied with coldness and some vanity. 'And my head would not be smashed.'

'You would not say so,' answered the Irishman. 'You would not say so.' His eyes sparkled with pure pleasure. 'You'd be dead.'

The boys laughed, but they looked at me with admiration.

Then, I do not know how or why, I began to see a difficulty. Without warning and as if I had gone into my bedroom at night and had found a gross ape seated in my bed and thereafter following me about with his grunts and his fleas and a look, relentless and ancient, scored on his brown face, I was faced with the problem that prowls at the centre of all religious faith. I was faced by the difficulty of the origin of evil. Evil was an illusion, we were taught. But even illusions have an origin. The Purifiers denied this.

I consulted my uncle. Trade was bad at the time and this made his faith abrupt. He frowned as I spoke.

'When did you brush your coat last?' he said. 'You're getting slovenly about your appearance. If you spent more time studying books' – that is to say, the Purification literature – 'and less with your hands in your pockets and playing about with boats on the river, you wouldn't be letting Error in.'

All dogmas have their jargon; my uncle as a businessman loved the trade terms of the Purification. 'Don't let Error in' was a favourite one. The whole point about the Purification, he said, was that it was scientific and therefore exact; in consequence it was sheer weakness to admit discussion. Indeed, betrayal. He unpinched his pince-nez, stirred his tea, and indicated I must submit or change the subject. Preferably the latter. I saw, to my alarm, that my arguments had defeated my uncle. Faith and doubt pulled like strings round my throat.

'You don't mean to say you don't believe that what our Lord said was true?' my aunt asked nervously, following me out of the room. 'Your uncle does, dear.'

I could not answer. I went out of the house and down the main street to the river, where the punts were stuck like insects in the summery flash of the reach. Life was a dream, I thought, no, a nightmare, for the ape was beside me.

I was still in this state, half sulking and half exalted, when Mr Hubert Timberlake came to the town. He was one of the important people from the headquarters of our church and he had come to give an address on the Purification at the Corn Exchange. Posters announcing this were everywhere. Mr Timberlake was to spend Sunday afternoon with us. It was unbelievable that a man so eminent would actually sit in our dining-room, use our knives and forks, and eat our food. Every imperfection in our home and our characters would jump out at him. The Truth had been revealed to man with scientific accuracy – an accuracy we could all test by experiment – and the future course of human development on earth was laid down, finally. And here in Mr Timberlake was a man who had not merely performed many miracles – even, it was said with proper reserve, having twice raised the dead – but had actually been to Toronto, our headquarters, where this great and revolutionary revelation had first been given.

'This is my nephew,' my uncle said, introducing me. 'He lives with us. He thinks he thinks, Mr Timberlake, but I tell him he only thinks he does. Ha, ha.' My uncle was a humorous man when he was with the great. 'He's always on the river,' my uncle continued. 'I tell him he's got water on the brain. I've been telling Mr Timberlake about you, my boy.'

A hand as soft as the best quality chamois leather took mine. I saw a wide upright man in a double-breasted navy-blue suit. He had a pink square head with very small ears and one of those torpid, enamelled smiles which were said by our enemies to be too common in our sect.

'Why, isn't that just fine?' said Mr Timberlake, who, owing to his contacts with Toronto, spoke with an American accent. 'What say we tell your uncle it's funny he thinks he's funny.'

The eyes of Mr Timberlake were direct and colourless. He had the look of a retired merchant captain who had become decontaminated from the sea and had reformed and made money. His defence of me had made me his at once. My doubts vanished. Whatever Mr Timberlake believed must be true, and as I listened to him at lunch, I thought there could be no finer life than his.

'I expect Mr Timberlake's tired after his address,' said my aunt.

'Tired?' exclaimed my uncle, brilliant with indignation. 'How can Mr Timberlake be tired? Don't let Error in!'

For in our faith the merely inconvenient was just as illusory as a great catastrophe would have been, if you wished to be strict, and Mr Timberlake's presence made us very strict.

I noticed then that, after their broad smiles, Mr Timberlake's lips had the habit of setting into a long depressed sarcastic curve.

'I guess,' he drawled, 'I guess the Al-mighty must have been tired sometimes, for it says He re-laxed on the seventh day. Say, do you know what I'd like to do this afternoon?' he said, turning to me. 'While your uncle and aunt are sleeping off this meal let's you and me go on the river and get water on the brain. I'll show you how to punt.'

Mr Timberlake, I saw to my disappointment, was out to show he understood the young. I saw he was planning a 'quiet talk' with me about my problems.

'There are too many people on the river on Sundays,' said my uncle uneasily.

'Oh, I like a crowd,' said Mr Timberlake, giving my uncle a tough look. 'This is the day of rest, you know.' He had had my uncle gobbling up every bit of gossip from the sacred city of Toronto all the morning.

My uncle and aunt were incredulous that a man like Mr Timberlake should go out among the blazers and gramophones of the river on a Sunday afternoon. In any other member of our church they would have thought this sinful.

'Waal, what say?' said Mr Timberlake. I could only murmur.

'That's fixed,' said Mr Timberlake. And on came the smile as simple, vivid, and unanswerable as the smile on an advertisement. 'Isn't that just fine!'

Mr Timberlake went upstairs to wash his hands. My uncle was deeply offended and shocked, but he could say nothing. He unpinched his glasses.

'A very wonderful man,' he said. 'So human,' he apologized.

'My boy,' my uncle said, 'this is going to be an experience for you. Hubert Timberlake was making a thousand a year in the insurance business ten years ago. Then he heard of the Purification. He threw everything up, just like that. He gave up his job and took up the work. It was a struggle, he told me so himself this morning. "Many's the time," he said to me this morning, "when I wondered where my next meal was coming from." But the way was shown. He came down from Worcester to London and in two years he was making fifteen hundred a year out of his practice.'

To heal the sick by prayer according to the tenets of the Church of the Last Purification was Mr Timberlake's profession.

My uncle lowered his eyes. With his glasses off, the lids were small and uneasy. He lowered his voice too.

'I have told him about your little trouble,' my uncle said quietly with emotion. I was burned with shame. My uncle looked up and stuck out his chin confidently.

'He just smiled,' my uncle said. 'That's all.'

Then we waited for Mr Timberlake to come down.

I put on white flannels and soon I was walking down to the river with Mr Timberlake. I felt that I was going with him under false pretences; for he would begin explaining to me the origin of evil and I would have to pretend politely that he was converting me when already, at the first sight of him, I had believed. A stone bridge, whose two arches were like an owlish pair of eyes gazing up the reach, was close to the landing-stage. I thought what a pity it was the flannelled men and the sunburned girls there did not know I was getting a ticket for *the* Mr Timberlake who had been speaking in the town that very morning. I looked round for him and when I saw him I was a little startled. He was standing at the edge of the water looking at it with an expression of empty incomprehension. Among the white crowds his air of brisk efficiency had dulled. He looked middle-aged, out of place, and insignificant. But the smile switched on when he saw me.

'Ready?' he called. 'Fine!'

I had the feeling that inside him there must be a gramophone record going round and round, stopping at that word.

He stepped into the punt and took charge.

'Now I just want you to paddle us over to the far bank,' he said, 'and then I'll show you how to punt.'

Everything Mr Timberlake said still seemed unreal to me. The fact that he was sitting in a punt, of all commonplace material things, was incredible. That he should propose to pole us up the river was terrifying. Suppose he fell into the river? At once I checked the thought. A leader of our church under the direct guidance of God could not possibly fall into a river.

The stream is wide and deep in this reach, but on the southern bank there is a manageable depth and a hard bottom. Over the clay banks the willows hang, making their basketwork print of sun and shadow on the water, while under the gliding boats lie cloudy, chloride caverns. The hoop-like branches of the trees bend down until their tips touch the water like fingers making musical sounds. Ahead in midstream, on a day sunny as this one was, there is a path of strong light which is hard to look at unless you half close your eyes, and down this path on the crowded Sundays go the launches with their parasols and their pennants; and also the rowboats with their beetle-leg oars, which seem to dig the sunlight out of the water as they rise. Upstream one goes, on and on between the gardens and then between fields kept for grazing. On the afternoon when Mr Timberlake and I went out to settle the question of the origin of evil, the meadows were packed densely with buttercups.

'Now,' said Mr Timberlake decisively when I had paddled to the other side. 'Now I'll take her.'

He got over the seat into the well at the stern.

'I'll just get you clear of the trees,' I said.

'Give me the pole,' said Mr Timberlake, standing up on the little platform and making a squeak with his boots as he did so. 'Thank you, sir. I haven't done this for eighteen years, but I can tell you, brother, in those days I was considered some poler.'

He looked round and let the pole slide down through his hands. Then he gave the first difficult push. The punt rocked pleasantly and we moved forward. I sat facing him, paddle in hand, to check any inward drift of the punt.

'How's that, you guys?' said Mr Timberlake, looking round at our eddies and drawing in the pole. The delightful water sished down it.

'Fine,' I said. Deferentially I had caught the word.

He went on to his second and his third strokes, taking too much water on his sleeve, perhaps, and uncertain in his steering, which I corrected, but he was doing well.

'It comes back to me,' he said. 'How am I doing?'

'Just keep her out from the trees,' I said.

'The trees?' he said.

'The willows,' I said.

'I'll do it now,' he said. 'How's that? Not quite enough? Well, how's this?'

'Another one,' I said. 'The current runs strong this side.'

'What? More trees?' he said. He was getting hot.

'We can shoot out past them,' I said. 'I'll ease us over with the paddle.'

Mr Timberlake did not like this suggestion.

'No, don't do that. I can manage it,' he said. I did not want to offend one of the leaders of our church, so I put the paddle down; but I felt I ought to have taken him farther along away from the irritation of the trees.

'Of course,' I said, 'we could go under them. It might be nice.'

'I think,' said Mr Timberlake, 'that would be a very good idea.'

He lunged hard on the pole and took us towards the next archway of willow branches.

'We may have to duck a bit, that's all,' I said.

'Oh, I can push the branches up,' said Mr Timberlake.

'It is better to duck,' I said.

We were gliding now quickly towards the arch; in fact, I was already under it.

'I think I should duck,' I said. 'Just bend down for this one.'

'What makes the trees lean over the water like this?' asked Mr Timberlake. 'Weeping willows – I'll give you a thought there. How Error likes to make us dwell on sorrow. Why not call them *laughing* willows?' discoursed Mr Timberlake as the branch passed over my head.

'Duck,' I said.

'Where? I don't see them,' said Mr Timberlake, turning round.

'No, your head,' I said. 'The branch,' I called.

'Oh, the branch. This one?' said Mr Timberlake, finding a branch just against his chest and he put out a hand to lift it. It is not easy to lift a willow branch and Mr Timberlake was surprised. He stepped back as it gently and firmly leaned against him. He leaned back and pushed from his feet. And he pushed too far. The boat went on, I saw Mr Timberlake's boots leave the stern as he took an unthoughtful step backwards. He made a last-minute grasp at a stronger and higher branch, and then there he hung a yard above the water, round as a blue damson that is ripe and ready, waiting only for a touch to make it fall. Too late with the paddle and shot ahead by the force of his thrust, I could not save him.

For a full minute I did not believe what I saw, indeed, our religion taught us never to believe what we saw. Unbelieving, I could not move. I gaped. The impossible had happened. Only a miracle, I found myself saying, could save him.

What was most striking was the silence of Mr Timberlake as he hung from the tree. I was lost between gazing at him and trying to get the punt out of the small branches of the tree. By the time I had got the punt out, there were several yards of water between us, and the soles of his boots were very near the water as the branch bent under his weight. Boats were passing at the time but no one seemed to notice us. I was glad about this. This was a private agony. A double chin had appeared on the face of Mr Timberlake and his head was squeezed between his shoulders and his hanging arms. I saw him blink and look up at the sky. His eyelids were pale like a chicken's. He was tidy and dignified as he hung there, the hat was not displaced, and the top button of his coat was done up. He had a blue silk handkerchief in his breast pocket. So unperturbed and genteel he seemed that as the tips of his shoes came nearer and nearer to the water, I became alarmed. He could perform what are called miracles. He would be thinking at this moment that only in an erroneous and illusory sense was he hanging from the branch of the tree over six feet of water. He was probably praying one of the closely reasoned prayers of our faith, which were more like conversations with Euclid than appeals to God. The calm of his face suggested this. Was he, I asked myself, within sight of the main road, the town recreation ground, and the landing-stage crowded with people, was he about to re-enact a well-known miracle? I hoped that he was not. I prayed that he was not. I prayed with all my will that Mr Timberlake would not walk upon the water. It was my prayer and not his that was answered.

I saw the shoes dip, the water rise above his ankles and up his socks. He tried to move his grip now to a yet higher branch

– he did not succeed – and in making this effort his coat and waistcoat rose and parted from his trousers. One seam of shirt with its pant-loops and brace-tabs broke like a crack across the middle of Mr Timberlake. It was like a fatal flaw in a statue, an earthquake crack that made the monumental mortal. The last Greeks must have felt as I felt then, when they saw a crack across the middle of some statue of Apollo. It was at this moment I realized that the final revelation about man and society on earth had come to nobody and that Mr Timberlake knew nothing at all about the origin of evil.

All this takes long to describe, but it happened in a few seconds as I paddled towards him. I was too late to get his feet on the boat and the only thing to do was to let him sink until his hands were nearer the level of the punt and then to get him to change hand-holds. Then I would paddle him ashore. I did this. Amputated by the water, first a torso, then a bust, then a mere head and shoulders, Mr Timberlake, I noticed, looked sad and lonely as he sank. He was a declining dogma. As the water lapped his collar – for he hesitated to let go of the branch to hold the punt – I saw a small triangle of deprecation and pathos between his nose and the corners of his mouth. The head resting on the platter of water had the sneer of calamity on it, such as one sees in the pictures of a beheaded saint.

'Hold on to the punt, Mr Timberlake,' I said urgently. 'Hold on to the punt.'

He did so.

'Push from behind,' he directed in a dry business-like voice. They were his first words. I obeyed him. Carefully I paddled him towards the bank. He turned and, with a splash, climbed ashore. There he stood, raising his arms and looking at the water running down his swollen suit and making a puddle at his feet.

'Say,' said Mr Timberlake coldly, 'we let some Error in that time.'

How much he must have hated our family.

'I am sorry, Mr Timberlake,' I said. 'I am most awfully sorry.

113

I should have paddled. It was my fault. I'll get you home at once. Let me wring out your coat and waistcoat. You'll catch your death –'

I stopped. I had nearly blasphemed. I had nearly suggested that Mr Timberlake had fallen into the water and that to a man of his age this might be dangerous.

Mr Timberlake corrected me. His voice was impersonal, addressing the laws of human existence rather than myself.

'If God made water it would be ridiculous to suggest He made it capable of harming His creatures. Wouldn't it?'

'Yes,' I murmured hypocritically.

'O.K.,' said Mr Timberlake. 'Let's go.'

'I'll soon get you across,' I said.

'No,' he said. 'I mean let's go on. We're not going to let a little thing like this spoil a beautiful afternoon. Where were we going? You spoke of a pretty landing-place farther on. Let's go there.'

'But I must take you home. You can't sit there soaked to the skin. It will spoil your clothes.'

'Now, now,' said Mr Timberlake. 'Do as I say. Go on.'

There was nothing to be done with him. I held the punt into the bank and he stepped in. He sat like a bursting and sodden bolster in front of me while I paddled. We had lost the pole, of course.

For a long time I could hardly look at Mr Timberlake. He was taking the line that nothing had happened and this put me at a disadvantage. I knew something considerable had happened. That glaze, which so many of the members of our sect had on their faces and persons, their minds and manners, had been washed off. There was no gleam for me from Mr Timberlake.

'What's the house over there?' he asked. He was making conversation. I had steered into the middle of the river to get him into the strong sun. I saw steam rise from him.

I took courage and studied him. He was a man, I realized, in poor physical condition, unexercised and sedentary. Now the gleam had left him, one saw the veined empurpled skin of the stoutish man with a poor heart. I remember he had said at lunch:

'A young woman I know said: "Isn't it wonderful? I can walk thirty miles in a day without being in the least tired." I said: "I don't see that bodily indulgence is anything a member of the Church of the Last Purification should boast about."'

Yes, there was something flaccid, passive, and slack about Mr Timberlake. Bunched in swollen clothes, he refused to take them off. It occurred to me, as he looked with boredom at the water, the passing boats, and the country, that he had not been in the country before. That it was something he had agreed to do but wanted to get over quickly. He was totally uninterested. By his questions – what is that church? Are there any fish in this river? Is that a wireless or a gramophone? – I understood that Mr Timberlake was formally acknowledging a world he did not live in. It was too interesting, too eventful a world. His spirit, inert and preoccupied, was elsewhere in an eventless and immaterial habitation. He was a dull man, duller than any man I had ever known; but his dullness was a sort of earthly deposit left by a being whose diluted mind was far away in the effervescence of metaphysical matters. There was a slightly pettish look on his face as (to himself, of course) he declared he was not wet and he would not have a heart attack or catch pneumonia.

Mr Timberlake spoke little. Sometimes he squeezed water out of his sleeve. He shivered a little. He watched his steam. I had planned, when we set out, to go up as far as the lock, but now the thought of another two miles of this responsibility was too much. I pretended I wanted to go only as far as the bend we were approaching, where one of the richest buttercup meadows was. I mentioned this to him. He turned and looked with boredom at the field. Slowly we came to the bank.

We tied up the punt and we landed.

'Fine,' said Mr Timberlake. He stood at the edge of the meadow just as he had stood at the landing-stage – lost, stupefied, uncomprehending.

'Nice to stretch our legs,' I said. I led the way into the deep flowers. So dense were the buttercups there was hardly any green. Presently I sat down. Mr Timberlake looked at me and sat down also. Then I turned to him with a last try at persuasion. Respectability, I was sure, was his trouble.

'No one will see us,' I said. 'This is out of sight of the river. Take off your coat and trousers and wring them out.'

Mr Timberlake replied firmly: 'I am satisfied to remain as I am. What is this flower?' he asked, to change the subject.

'Buttercup,' I said.

'Of course,' he replied.

I could do nothing with him. I lay down full length in the sun; and, observing this and thinking to please me, Mr Timberlake did the same. He must have supposed that this was what I had come out in the boat to do. It was only human. He had come out with me, I saw, to show me that he was only human.

But as we lay there I saw the steam still rising. I had had enough.

'A bit hot,' I said, getting up.

He got up at once.

'Do you want to sit in the shade?' he asked politely.

'No,' I said. 'Would you like to?'

'No,' he said. 'I was thinking of you.'

'Let's go back,' I said. We both stood up and I let him pass in front of me. When I looked at him again, I stopped dead. Mr Timberlake was no longer a man in a navy-blue suit. He was blue no longer. He was transfigured. He was yellow. He was covered with buttercup pollen, a fine yellow paste of it made by the damp, from head to foot.

'Your suit,' I said.

He looked at it. He raised his thin eyebrows a little, but he did not smile or make any comment.

The man is a saint, I thought. As saintly as any of those gold-leaf figures in the churches of Sicily. Golden he sat in the punt; golden he sat for the next hour as I paddled him down the river.

Golden and bored. Golden as we landed at the town and as we walked up the street back to my uncle's house. There he refused to change his clothes or to sit by a fire. He kept an eye on the time for his train back to London. By no word did he acknowledge the disasters or the beauties of the world. If they were printed upon him, they were printed upon a husk.

Sixteen years have passed since I dropped Mr Timberlake in the river and since the sight of his pant-loops destroyed my faith. I have not seen him since, but today I heard that he was dead. He was fifty-seven. His mother, a very old lady with whom he had lived all his life, went into his bedroom when he was getting ready for church and found him lying on the floor in his shirt-sleeves. A stiff collar with the tie half inserted was in one hand. Five minutes before, she told the doctor, she had been speaking to him.

The doctor, who looked at the heavy body lying on the single bed, saw a middle-aged man, wide rather than stout and with an extraordinary box-like thick-jawed face. He had got fat, my uncle told me, in later years. The heavy liver-coloured cheeks were like the chaps of a hound. Heart disease, it was plain, was the cause of the death of Mr Timberlake. In death the face was lax, even coarse and degenerate. It was a miracle, the doctor said, that he had lived as long. Any time during the last twenty years the smallest shock might have killed him.

I thought of our afternoon on the river. I thought of him hanging from the tree. I thought of him indifferent and golden in the meadow. I understood why he had made for himself a protective, sedentary blandness, an automatic smile, a collection of phrases. He kept them on like the coat after his ducking. And I understood why – though I had feared it all the time we were on the river – I understood why he did not talk to me about the origin of evil. He was honest. The ape was with us. The ape that merely followed me was already inside Mr Timberlake eating out his heart.

A Time to Keep

Alan Sillitoe

MARTIN DREW THE cloth from the kitchen table. An old tea-stain made a map of Greenland when held up to the light. He folded it into an oblong and laid it on the dresser.

After the anxiety of getting his brother and sister to bed he lifted his books from the cupboard and spread them over the bare wood, where they would stay till the heart-catching click of the gate latch signalled his parents' return.

He was staying in to see that the fire did not go out, and to keep the light on. He was staying up because he was older. When that unmistakable click of the gate latch sounded he would set a kettle on the gas to make coffee. Funny how thirsty they still were after being in the boozer all night. His two-hour dominion over the house would be finished, but as consolation he could give in to the relief of knowing that they had not after all been hit by a bus and killed.

Most of the books had been stolen. None had been read from end to end. When opened they reeked of damp from bookshop shelves. Or they stank from years of storage among plant pots and parlour soot.

He put a French grammar on to *Peveril of the Peak*, and a Bible in Polish on top of that. The clock could be heard now that they were out and he had extinguished the television. He sang a tune to its ticking under his breath, then went back to his books. He would start work next year, and didn't know whether he wanted to or not. Things could go on like this for ever as far as he was concerned. You got booted out of school though, at fifteen, and that was that.

The certainty that one day he would be pushed into a job had hovered around him since he first realized as a child that his father went out every morning in order to earn money with which to feed them, pay the rent, get clothes, and keep a roof over their heads. His mother used these phrases, and they stabbed into him like fire. At that time work had nothing to do with him, but it soon would have. It was a place of pay and violence which his father detested, to judge by the look on his face when he came home every evening with his snapsack and teacan.

Under the dark space of the stairs he shovelled around for coal to bank up the dull fire – a pleasurable task, as long as the flames came back to life. A hole in the pan needed bigger lumps set over it so that cobbles and slack wouldn't spill on the mat between the coal-heap and grate. They'd rather have a few pints of beer than buy a dustpan.

He washed his hands in the scullery. He liked soap that was keen to the smell. Arranging his chair, he sat down again and lifted the cover of a beige leather-bound volume of French magazines. He read a sentence under the picture: a bridge over the River Seine near Rouen. In other books he was able to put Portuguese or Italian phrases into English. When a word appealed to his sight he manoeuvred through the alphabet of a dictionary to get at its meaning, though he never tried to learn a language properly. He handled books like a miser. In each one his name was written in capital letters, though there was no danger of them being stolen, because they were gold that could not be spent. The strange kind of hunger he felt in looking at them often fixed him into a hypnosis that stopped him using them properly.

If burglars came they would nick the television, not books. They were stacked according to size, then sorted in their various languages. Excitement led him to range them from high at both ends to small in the middle. He bracketed them between a tea-caddy and a box of his father's car tools so that none could escape. Then he spread them out again, like playing cards.

Summer was ending. It seemed as if it always was. He had a bike, but Friday night was too much of a treat to go out. He also thought it a squander of precious daylight on his parents' part that they should have been in the pub for an hour before it got dark. And yet, as soon as the outside walls and chimney pots were no longer clear, he swung the curtains decisively together, pushing away what little of the day was left. Once it was going, he wanted to be shut of it. He switched on glowing light that made the living room a secret cave no one could get into.

His parents were used to his daft adoration of books, but for anyone beyond the family to witness his vital playthings would make him blush with shame. Aunts, cousins and uncles would mock him, but what else could you expect? If it hadn't been that, they'd have teased him for something else. They had never actually seen his books, though they had been laughingly told about them by his parents. Books and the people he knew didn't belong together, and that was a fact, but he knew it was impossible to live without either.

He wondered what other eyes had slid across these pages. Their faces could be frightening, or happy. They had come in out of the rain after doing a murder. Or they closed a book and put it down so as to go out and do a good deed. How did you know? You never did. You had to make it all up and scare yourself daft.

In any case, how had they felt about what they were reading? What houses had they lived in, and what sort of schools had they gone to? Did they like their furniture? Did they hate their children? He would rather have been any one of those people than himself. Maybe nobody had read the books. They got them as presents, or bought them and forgot to read them. The thought made him feel desolate, though not for long. Books always took his mind off the world around. He lifted the picture-album of France, and pondered on every voyage the book had made. It had been to Chile and China, and all the other places he could think of, between leaving the printers and reaching his table in Radford.

A clatter of footsteps at the yardend and the boisterous notes of a voice he did not at first recognize dragged him clear. Print had hooks, but they were made of rubber. Before the warning click of the gate latch his dozen volumes were scooped off the table and stacked on the floor behind the far side of the dresser.

By the time the door opened the gas was lit and a full kettle set on it. He put sugar, milk and a bottle of coffee on the table, then sat looking through a car magazine as if he hadn't moved all evening. His cousin Raymond was first in the room. No stranger, after all. His mother and father breathed a strong smell of ale.

'He's the quickest lad I know at getting that kettle on the burning feathers!' his father said. 'A real marvel at it. I drove like a demon back from the Crown for my cup o' coffee.'

'And you nearly hit that van coming out of Triumph Road,' Raymond laughed.

Martin wondered whether he should take such praise as it was intended, or hate his father for imagining that he needed it, or despise him for thinking he could get round him in such a way. He was already taller than his father, and there were times when he couldn't believe it, and occasions when he didn't like it, though he knew he had to get used to it. So had his father, but he didn't seem bothered by such a thing. He decided to ignore the praise, though he *had* got the kettle on in record time.

'You brought him up right,' Raymond hung his jacket on the back of the door. 'He worn't drug up, like me.' He bumped into his aunt: 'Oops, duck, mind yer back, yer belly's in danger!'

Martin laughed, without knowing whether he wanted to or not. His father would put up with anything from Raymond, who had been to Approved School, Detention Centre and Borstal, though he was now an honest man of twenty-two, and able to charm anybody when he wanted. He did it so well that you were convinced he would never get caught stealing again. He could also use a bullying, jocular sort of self-confidence, having learned how to live rough, half-inch a thing or two, and die young if he must, without getting sent down every year for a Christmas box or birthday present. Another lesson well taken was that he must always look smart, talk clear and act quick, so that anyone who mattered would think he could be trusted.

At Borstal he had done boxing, because it seemed that both God and the Governor were on the side of those who stored the deadliest punch. He had developed one as fast as he could, and wasn't afraid to use it whenever necessary. He was loyal to his family, helping them with money and goods to the best of his ability and hard work. He was often heard to say that he couldn't go back to his old ways, for his mother's sake.

Martin wanted to be like his cousin, though sensing that he might never be so made him look up to him even more. He was certainly glad he'd got the books out of sight before he came in.

Raymond, with his bread and cheese, and cup of coffee, was first to sit down. Martin moved across the room, leaving the fire to the grown ups. The yellow flames blazed for them alone, and for their talk that came from the big world of boozers that he hadn't yet entered but was avid to. Raymond stretched out a leg, and expertly belched the words: 'Pardon me!' – at which they all laughed.

He held his cup for more coffee. 'I'll be off to Alfreton again in the morning. Help to build another mile o' that motorway. You know how it's done, don't you? I open my big gob wide. Somebody shovels tar and concrete in. Then I walk along shitting out motorway and coughing up signposts!'

'It'll soon be as far as Leeds, wain't it?' his father said quickly, trying to head off such remarks, which he found a bit too loud-mouthed.

Raymond detected the manoeuvre, and to save face, turned censorious: 'It would be, Joe, if everybody got cracking at their job. But they're too busy looting to get much done. The fields for miles on either side are laid waste by plundering navvies. Some of 'em sit around smoking and talking, and waiting for a turnip to show itself above the soil. As soon as it does, up it comes! They go straight into their snapsacks.'

He was a joker. They weren't sure whether it was true or not. No gaffer could afford to let you get away with not working full-tilt. But he *had* brought vegetables home. Ripping up a basketful was the work of a few minutes in the dusk: 'A bloke the other day come to wok in his minivan,' Raymond told them, 'and drove it a little way into the wood. He kept the engine running so's we wouldn't hear his chainsaw, but when I went in for a piss I saw the bleeder stacking logs in the back. A nice young pine tree had gone, and he covered the stump up wi' leaves. Nowt's safe. It's bleddy marvellous. He's going to get caught one day, doing it in the firm's time!'

Martin seemed born to listen. Maybe it went with collecting books. If he read them properly he'd perhaps start talking a bit more, and it might be easier then to know what other people were thinking.

'He don't say much,' Raymond observed, 'our Martin don't, does he?'

But he did at school. Among his pals he was as bright as an Amazon parrot. If he tackled a book properly, on the other hand, he might talk even less. It was hard to say until he did. Cut anybody's finger off who got too fresh. The teacher once stopped him bashing up another boy, and said if he caught him at it again he'd pull his arm off. He couldn't really be like Raymond, who'd once got chucked out of school for hitting a teacher right between the eyes.

'He'll be at work next year,' his mother nodded at Martin. 'It's looney to keep 'em till they're fifteen, big kids like him. Give him summat to do. *And* bring us some money in.'

'The bloody road tax is twenty-five quid now,' his father said bitterly, and Martin felt as if he were being blamed for it.

'I didn't have one for six months last year,' Raymond boasted. 'I stuck an old Guinness label on the windscreen. Nobody twigged it.'

Martin knew it wasn't true.

'You never did!' his father said, who believed it. 'I wish I'd had such an idea.'

'No, I tell a lie. It was only on for a fortnight. Then I got the wind up, and brought a real 'un.' He turned his grey eyes on to Martin, as if embarrassed by somebody who didn't continually give themselves away in speech. 'I'll get our Martin a job wi' me on the motorway, though,' he said. 'That'll settle his hash. He'll come home every night absolutely knackered.'

I expect I might, Martin thought. 'What would I do?'

'You'd have to get up early, for a start.'

That wouldn't bother him. Lots of people did. 'What time's that?'

'Six.'

'He's dead to the wide at six. It's all I can do to get him out of bed by eight o'clock.'

'I'm not, our mam.'

Raymond looked at the fire, as if he would have spat at the bars if it had been in his own home. 'I pass here in my car at half past. I'll pick you up tomorrow, if you like.'

'Will yer be fit for it?' his father wanted to know.

Martin, taking more coffee and another slice of bread, didn't think he'd heard right. He often looked at the opening of a book, and when he understood every word, couldn't believe he'd read it properly, and then went back to make sure. 'Tomorrow?'

'Well, I din't say owt about yesterday, did I?'

If Raymond said something, he meant it. He often said that you must regret nothing, and that you should always keep promises. It helped his reputation of being a man who showed up in a crowd. So he promised something in a loud voice now and again in order to keep himself up to scratch. 'I'll stop my owd banger outside the Co-op. If you're there I'll take you. If you ain't, I'll just push on.'

'I'll be waiting.' Martin felt like one of those sailors in the olden days who, about to set off west, wasn't sure he would ever get back again.

The sky was clear and cold. He saw it over the housetops, and above the façade of the bingo hall that he first went into as a cinema one Saturday afternoon nearly ten years ago.

The wet road looked as clean as if a light shone on it. He buttoned the jacket over his shirt. You never wore a top coat to work unless you were one of the older men. It was too early for traffic, making the road look different to when it was pounded by buses and lorries during the day. His mother had disturbed him from a hundred feet under the sand below the deepest part of the ocean when she had tried to wake him. She had to grab the clothes off him in the end.

Sandwiches bulged in his pocket. He enjoyed waiting, but his hands were cold. 'Never put your hands in your pockets when you're on the job,' Raymond had said. 'A lot of 'em do, but it don't look good.' He couldn't do it while waiting to go there, either. He wished he were setting off to work properly, and that he didn't have another year to do before he got real wages. There wasn't much point in starting work today, and then next year as well.

A postman went by on a bike. 'Morning, kid.'

'Morning.'

Raymond's car had rust along the bottom of the door as it swung open towards him. 'Get in.'

He sounded disappointed that Martin had been able to meet him. The car sailed up Wollaton Road like an aeroplane, spun around the traffic island by the Crown, and went along Western Boulevard. 'Tired?'

'It's a treat, being up early.'

'Bring owt t'eat?'

'Yeh. Mam forgot some tea, though.'

'I've got a mashing.' He played the car with hands and feet as if on a big picture-house organ. 'Sugar, tea, and tinned milk – solid like a cannon ball. Enough for a battalion. Trust our mam. She's old-fashioned, but she's a marvel all the same. You can stand a garden fork in *her* strong tea.'

Beyond the town there was a cloud like a big white dog. Martin yawned, and expected it to do the same.

'We like to start as soon as daylight hits,' Raymond went on. 'That's where the money is, in overtime. You don't mind getting out o' yer warm bed when you can mek a bit of money. I'd wok all hours God sends, for money. Watch the tax, though. Bastards will skin you dry, and fry you rotten. Dangerous work, as well. Nearly got scooped up by a mechanical digger the other day. But it's money that I like to be getting into my pocket, fartin' Martin! As soon as I know there's money to be earned I'd dig that soil up with my fingernails. They don't need to tell *me* when to start sweating!'

Martin had a question. 'What do you do with it?'

'Wi' what?'

'The money you get.'

'Ah! Booze a bit – that's me. Treat everybody – now and again. Save a lot, though. Gonna buy a house when I've got the deposit. Me and mam'll live in it. Not the other spongers, though. They wain't get a look in.'

His brothers and sisters had reputations as scroungers. Serve 'em right if Raymond dealt with them as they deserved.

The narrow lane was so rutted he thought they'd get stuck, the car swaying from side to side, sharp privet branches scraping the window. The wheels skidded on the mud in a couple of places, but it didn't bother Raymond. He steered as if in a rally car, then grumbled: 'Fuckers should have cut that hedge down' – seeing in his mirror another car grinding too closely behind.

As they topped the rise tears of muddy water lashed against the windscreen. When the wipers flushed over it Martin saw the vast clayey cutting between green banks. It was a man-made valley occupied by lorries, cranes, mechanical diggers. Those already moving seemed to be the ones that owned it. He was surprised at how few men there were, having expected to see them swarming all over the place.

Raymond drove parallel to the valley, and parked his car by a cluster of huts. He got out, and farted, then stretched his arms and legs. 'See that trailer?'

'Yes.'

'Well, I'm going to book myself in.'

The nearest wooden hut, full of tools, smelt as if it were made of still-growing trees. He expected to tread on leaves as he went in to have a look, but there was a crunch of gravel under his boots. His eyes were sore from little sleep. He yawned while trying to stretch his arms without being seen.

The sound of engines moaned and jerked from the canyon. They formed a chorus. There was never silence. Raw earth was being cleared. Soon it would be covered, and packed, and solidified, and paved to take traffic and huge lorries between London and Leeds. The men who did it knew what their work was for. They could see it as plain as a streak of paint across a piece of new wood. But it must go so slowly that a month was like a day.

Raymond came back wearing a helmet and a livid pink jacket. 'Don't stand idle,' he called sharply, so that Martin didn't know whether he was joking or not. 'Let's get on that motor.'

The dumper truck swayed as it went down the track hewn in the incline. The narrow ledge frightened him, for the dumper might tumble any minute and take both of them to the bottom. Raymond fought with the wheel and gears, laughed and swore as he swung it zig-zag along.

'This fucking thing – it's like a dog: I tamed it a long while ago, so you've no need to worry.' The machine went more quickly. 'If we don't get down in one piece, though, I'll get the push. That's the sort of world we're living in, Martin. Owt happens to this dumper, and I get my cards. Don't matter about us, if we get killed. We'll get compo, but what good does that do yer?'

He drove the petrol-smelling truck under the digger to take its load, then lumbered it back up the escarpment in such a way that Martin didn't think he'd tamed it at all. Tipping it from above helped to heighten the embankment: 'The bleeding gaffer wanted to know what *you* was doing here, so I told him you was the new mash-lad from Cresswell. He's got so much on his plate though, that gaffer, that he don't know whether he's coming or going. Looked a bit gone-out at me, burree din't say owt.'

After two trips Martin decided to stay on top. He could watch the beetling dumpers doing their work from a distance, which was better than being down among them. He remembered a word from school that would describe the long deep scar: geology, geological. The layers of gravel and grit and clay were being sliced like a cake so that the motorway could be pushed through into Yorkshire.

In a while he sat down. It was a struggle to keep the eyes open when you weren't thinking about anything. The wind died and the sun came out. He was dozing in its warm beams, then dreaming, but he never cut off from the distant punch and rumble of machinery, and the occasional shouting that broke through as if finding him at the end of a long search.

Diesel smoke wafted across. He opened his eyes so as not to lose contact with the sort of work he hoped to be getting paid for next year. Raymond nudged him awake: 'You poor bogger! A bit too early in the morning, was it?'

'No, it worn't,' he snapped.

'You know why, though, don't you?' He had a can of hot tea, and offered him the lid as a cup. 'Take this. I'll get some scoff.'

'Why?' The sweet strong tea went straight to the waking-up box behind his eyes.

'You stayed up too late. Can't go to work early if you don't get to your wanking pit on time. Not unless you're over eighteen, anyway. You'll 'ave to stop reading all them books. Send you blind.'

He'd heard that before – often. 'I'm not tired.'

Raymond rolled a neat cigarette. 'What about some snout, then?'

'No thanks.'

He laughed. Smoke drifted from his open mouth. 'That's right. Keep off the fags. Don't booze, either, or go with women. Stick to your books as long as you can. And you know why? I'll tell yer: because fags pack your lungs in, booze softens your brain, and women give you the clap.'

With that, he went back to work.

Martin didn't know what to make of such advice, so it didn't seem important. He wished he had one of the books he'd stacked and shifted about on the table last night, even if it was only the Bible in Polish, or the Italian dictionary. When dumper trucks again moved into the canyon, and the first one came back loaded, they didn't interest him any more, though he thought they might if he sat at the wheel of one like Raymond.

An hour later he was so bored that he felt hungry, so finished off his last cheese sandwich. Sitting high up and set apart gave him a picture-view. Nothing happened, and he was bored, yet everything moved so slowly that he wouldn't forget it as long as he lived.

Raymond's truck was easy to recognize. He saw clearly across the whole distance, and watched him go with his load up the far slope of the motorway. A wind blew from the street of a town on the skyline, as if someone on the church top in the middle were wafting it over. With his vivid sight he saw Raymond's truck go behind a long spoil bank, the helmet moving slowly. Then his body reappeared, and finally the truck again.

It was manoeuvred into a clearing for about the twentieth time, and guided close to the escarpment by another man. It waited a few seconds, as if to get breath, then it tipped its load. There was no pause before setting off quickly towards the excavation for another.

He stared more closely, imagining he was Raymond sitting on the truck and working the levers, confidently steering after four years' experience, smelling old oil and new soil and wondering how much he would coin that day. He wouldn't mind working here, even if he did have to start by seeing to the men's tea and running errands from one hut to another. A mash-lad was better than a school-kid.

The truck reversed towards the precipice at a normal and careful speed. At dusk they'd drive back to Nottingham. Maybe Raymond would call at home for a bite to eat before going to where he lived in the Meadows – though it wasn't likely because he never went visiting in his working clothes.

He could almost hear the engines speeding up. 'I'll get this one over with,' Raymond might be saying, 'then I'll pack it in and piss off out of it. Done enough graft for one day.' He sensed the words going through his brain. He said them aloud, as if to save his cousin the thought or energy.

He couldn't say who was tired most: him, Raymond, or the man whom Raymond's dumper truck knocked flying over the almost sheer slope. The man had sauntered out of the way as usual but then, for a reason which was hard to make out (though he was sure there must have been one, since there always was a reason – for everything), he leapt back against the truck as if to dive underneath.

It wasn't easy to decide the exact point of impact. The man's spade turned in the air, and Martin swore he heard the clatter as its metal head caught the side of the truck.

The body rolled down the steep banks and smashed into a mechanical digger. He watched Raymond jump from his seat. Other men lined the top of the spoil heap. Two or three, Raymond clearly among them, started to scramble down.

The whole heart-side of Martin's body was dulled with pain. It lasted a few seconds, then left him feeling cold, wind-blown and gritty at the eyes, which now seemed to lose their vision. The sound of an ambulance came from far away as he walked towards the huts. His legs and arms shivered as if from cold. He gripped himself till it stopped. The flashing blue lights of a police dar bobbed along the hedge-top.

He noticed how pale Raymond was when he got into the car an hour after his usual knocking-off time. He smoked a cigarette, something he said he never did when driving. 'That pig-copper told me I'd killed 'im on purpose,' he shouted above the engine as it roared and sent the car skidding along the muddy lane. 'They said I must have been larking about.'

'I didn't see yer, and I was watching.'

'A few others was as well, so I'm all right for witnesses. But can you believe it? Killed 'im on purpose! One of the blokes I'd known for weeks! Can you imagine him asking a thing like that?

Must be rotten to the bloody core. He just jumped in front of my truck.'

Martin felt as if he was asking the only question in his life that needed a proper answer:

'Why did he do it?'

After half a minute's silence, which seemed so long that Martin thought his cousin would never speak again, unless to tell him to mind his own business, Raymond said: 'You won't guess. Nobody on this earth would. I'll tell yer, though. He dropped his packet o' fags in front of my truck, and because he thought the wheels would crush 'em, he jumped to pick 'em up. The daft bastard didn't want to lose his fags. Would you believe it? Didn't *think*! Blokes who don't think deserve all they get. I'd have given him half of my own fags though, if only he'd left 'em alone.' He smiled bleakly at his untested generosity. 'Can't understand him doing a thing like that. I thought I knew him, but bogger me if I did. You don't know anybody, *ever*, Martin. So never think you do.'

'He's dead now, though.'

'The daft bleeder.'

Martin said he was sorry it happened. He hated feeling the tears at his eyes as sharp as glass. 'Who was he?'

'An old chap, about forty-odd. Happy old chokker. He was allus singing, he was. You could tell from his mouth, but nobody ever *heard* him because of the engines kicking up such a noise. He didn't sing when he thought we could hear him. Funny bloke altogether. All my life I've been careful, though, that's the best on it. I never wanted that to happen. I'm not a murderer, it don't matter what that copper tried to say. "I'm not a murderer, your honour! Honest, I'm not!" That's what I'll shout out in court when the case comes up.'

Back in the lighted streets, Martin said nothing. He had nothing to say, because everything had been *done*. His cousin drove with one hand, and held his wrist tight when he reached across with the other. 'I'm glad you came to work with me today, any road up, our Martin. I wouldn't have liked to drive home on my own after that little lot. I'll tek you right to your door. Don't say owt to your mam and dad, though, will yer?'

'Why?'

'Let me tell 'em, tomorrer.' He was on the edge of crying. Martin never thought he'd feel sorry for Raymond, but he did now. He felt more equal than he'd ever done – and even more than that. There wasn't much to look up to. The big mauler was crushing his wrist. 'Aren't you going to the boozer with them tonight?'

He drew his hand off, to change gear before stopping at the White Horse traffic lights. 'I think I'll get off home. Mam might go out and get me a bottle of ale from the beer-off.' He winked. 'If I ask her nice.'

Nothing could keep him down for long.

Martin wasn't as tired as he had been by the motorway. When his parents drove to the boozer he got his books out of the dresser, instead of going to the last house at the pictures as was usual on Saturday night.

The clear clean print was a marvel to his eyes. He started to read the first page, then became so drawn into the book that he didn't even hear the click of the gate latch when it sounded three hours later.

The Travellers

Stan Barstow

WHO THEY WERE, where they had come from and where they were going, I never did find out. There were times afterwards, in memory, when they seemed unreal; though they were real enough and welcome that night as they filed into the waiting-room out of the November fog which had clamped down on the country from coast to coast, disrupting my planned journey by bus and sending me to the little out-of-the-way junction to wait for the last train to the city, fifteen miles away.

There were about twenty of them; a nondescript bunch of sober, respectable men and women of varying ages. They crowded into one end of the narrow room, surrounding and hiding the heavy bare table as they huddled in their topcoats and made wry jokes about the weather outside. One man stood out from the rest by virtue of his dress as well as his general demeanour. He seemed to be in a position of authority or respon-sibility towards the others: in some way their leader; and they regarded him with restrained amusement as well as respect. He had already spoken to me as they came in, making some conventional remark about the state of the night, and now I looked at him with interest.

He was a small man with a red fleshy face and pince-nez perched on his fat little nose. He wore a dove-grey homburg hat tipped back from his forehead and his navy-blue double breasted overcoat hung open to reveal a blue polka-dot bow tie and a fawn waistcoat. But what really took my eyes were the felt spats which showed below the turn-ups of his grey-striped trousers. It was a long time since I'd seen a man in spats. He had altogether rather an air about him; a presence and a sense of dash exemplified by his clothes and the expansiveness of his gestures, which latter were no doubt heightened by the contents of the flat half-bottle of whisky whose neck protruded from one of the pockets of his overcoat.

I'd not been alone the entire time before this invasion. One would have expected any infusion of extra human warmth to alleviate the cheerless atmosphere of that bare room, but the entry of these earlier people, ten minutes after my arrival, had seemed to lower the temperature rather than raise it.

There were three of them: a middle-aged couple and an old man, tall and lean as a garden rake, who walked between them. The younger man had answered my good evening but the woman's response was to pierce me with a gimlet look, as though she suspected me of being an exponent of the three-card trick out to fleece them of their money, or a salesman who would spend the waiting-time unloading on to them fifteen volumes of an expensive and unwanted encyclopaedia.

Since then there had been no communication between us, not even the crossing of a glance. At the entrance of the little man's group they were still sitting motionless on the bench near the fireless gate, the couple like sentinels, one on each side of the old man, who seemed to be sunk in a coma, totally unaware of his surroundings, his gaze fixed on the floor some distance beyond the polished toes of his black boots. A narrow band of black material encircled the grey herring-bone tweed of his left arm. The woman was looking disapprovingly towards the crowded end of the room from behind round spectacles. I guessed she was a woman who looked disapprovingly at most things.

It had struck me a few minutes after their appearance that the group must be a choir, for they all carried bound copies of what looked like music. And as if to confirm my guess the little man now lifted his voice and addressed them all.

'We've got a while to wait, so what about a song to keep us warm?' There was a general murmur of assent followed by good-humoured groans and jeers as the little chap went on, 'Not that any chance to practise comes amiss, eh?'

He stood before them, his shoulders thrown back, regarding them with an almost comical assurance. He could handle them, I thought. He might be a slightly humorous figure but he knew how to deal with them.

'Well, sort yourselves out, then,' he said. 'Let's not get sloppy, because an audience is an audience, however small.' He half-turned and bowed his head in acknowledgment of our presence as the members of the choir reshuffled themselves and waited for his signal to begin. He pondered for a moment, then announced a piece whose name I didn't recognise, and the choir fell silent as he raised his arms.

It was as they burst into song that the old man's head lifted and turned. Something came to life in his eyes and the long fingers of each hand slowly clenched and unclenched themselves. The music was open-throated and stirring, designed to display the blend of the full choir, and the conductor guided it with flamboyant but accurate sweeps of his hands, his head cocked back and an expression of ecstasy on his plump shining face.

The old man suddenly stirred and got up, and before his companions had realised it he was striding down the room to stand at the end of the line of tenors. His head came up and his throat vibrated as he joined his voice to the singing.

The couple exchanged surprised glances and the woman said something to the man, her mouth snapping peevishly shut at the end of it. The man glanced uncertainly at the body of singers and the woman gave him a dig of the elbow which brought him to his feet. He crossed the room and took the old man's elbow and tried to lead him away. The old man was now singing at the pitch of his voice and the sound carried clear and wavering above that of the other singers. He shrugged the younger man off and the other said something to him and took his arm again.

Just then the conductor noticed the little scene and called out over the choir, 'Let him alone. He's all right. Singing does you good. It's a tonic.'

This seemed to nonplus the younger man and he stood for a moment looking uncomfortable before returning to his seat. The woman gave him a furious look as he sat down, and made as if to rise herself. But he restrained her with his hand and his lips formed the words, 'Leave him alone. He's all right.'

The woman went off into a long muttered harangue during which the man looked sheepishly at the floor. Then she nudged him as though to prod him into action again as the choir came to the end of their piece and the conductor applauded vigorously, shouting, 'Bravo, bravo! Lovely, lovely!' He took the whisky bottle out of his pocket and tilted it to his mouth.

'Now then,' he said. 'What about another one, eh. What this time? I know, I know. An old one. A real old favourite. *Love's old sweet song.*'

A moment later, before the little conductor could gather his importance round him and lift his arms, the old man had started the song in the still true, still sweet, but weak and quavering relic of what must, years before, have been a telling tenor voice:

' "Oft in the dear dead days beyond recall . . ." '

And the conductor, recovering from his momentary surprise, gazed fondly at the old man, holding back the choir until the chorus and then bringing them in, deep and sweet and rich:

' "Just a song at twilight, when the lights are low, and the flickering shadows softly come and go . . ." '

I watched and listened, my spine cold. For the old song had associations with my life, bringing memories of my mother's contralto voice and the gaiety and fun of family parties, so long ago . . .

' "Comes love's sweet song, comes lo-oves old swe-et song . . ." '

The music died into a hush. No one spoke or moved for several moments. The old man stood absolutely still, staring somewhere before him. Then the woman nudged her companion again and he went over and touched the old man's arm. The old man came this time, unresisting, and as he turned fully towards me I saw that his face was livid with emotion, his eyes bright and shining in the waiting-room lights. He was two steps from his seat when it all left him in a sudden draining of life and energy that took the use from his limbs and sent him slumping to the floor. At that moment too there was the clank of the loco outside and the porter stuck his head in at the door.

'This is it. The last one tonight.'

The choir broke their ranks and moved out in a body. As the little conductor brushed by some instinct made me reach out and lightly lift the whisky bottle from his pocket. The couple had got the old man on to the bench but he hadn't come round. I went over to them.

'Come on,' I said, 'I'll help you to get him on to the train.'

With his arms round our shoulders the younger man and I carried him between us to the waiting train and struggled him into a compartment where we laid him out on the seat. The woman got in behind us, clucking with exasperation. The porter slammed the door, a whistle sounded and the train jerked into motion.

'I knew we never should have come,' the woman said. 'I knew from the start 'at it was foolish; but he would have his way. And now look at him. It might be the end of him.'

I got the whisky bottle out. 'Hold his head up,' I said to the man, who was gazing helplessly at the prostrate figure on the seat. He put his arm under the old man's head and raised it.

'He's teetotal, y'know,' the woman said, looking at the whisky. 'He never touches strong drink.'

'He's ill too,' I said. 'It won't do him any harm.'

I put the bottle to the old man's lips and let a few drops of whisky trickle into his mouth, at the same time slipping my other hand inside his coat to feel for his heart.

'Wrap your overcoat up and put it under his head,' I said to the younger man.

The woman leaned forward from the opposite seat, the lenses of her glasses glinting in the light. 'Are you a doctor?' she said.

I said no, letting a few more drops of whisky trickle into the old man's throat. His breathing was becoming stronger.

'Will he be all right?' the man asked and I nodded. 'I think he's coming round now.'

We sat in a row and looked at the old man.

'I knew we never should have come,' the woman said again, and the man rubbed the palms of his hands nervously together between his knees.

I put the whisky away to give back to the little conductor when we got off the train. I imagined he'd be missing it by now.

'All that way,' the woman said. 'Thirty mile there and thirty mile back. And a cemetery on the doorstep! I told him but he wouldn't listen. Stupid. Stubborn.'

'He's her father,' the man said to me. 'We've been to bury his wife. Not her mother; his second wife. She came from up Clibden. Happen you know it.'

'A little place, up on the moors, isn't it?'

'That's right. Miles from anywhere. He met her while he was out hiking one day. They used to laugh about it together and say, how near he'd come to missing her. He'd reckon he wished he'd taken another turning. "I never knew what wa' waiting for me up that lane," he used to say.'

His voice sank to a confidential whisper. 'The wife, y'know, she didn't approve of the trip. She said we should've buried her nearer home, in the family grave. But he said he'd always promised to take her back there if she went first. We never thought he'd go through with it, it being winter an' all that. But we couldn't budge him. We never should've humoured him, though. The wife's right: we should've made him bury her at home. It's been too much for him. I don't suppose he'll ever be right again now . . . An' all that singin' . . . Whatever made him do a thing like that, d'you think? After he's been to a funeral, eh? I thought the wife 'ud die of shame when he got up like that and sang at the top of his voice.'

I looked at the old man as his son-in-law's voice droned fretfully on and thought of him in the waiting-room, singing the old songs . . . 'Just a song at twilight, when the lights are low . . .'

Then the woman spoke up suddenly from the other side of her husband. 'The trouble with old people,' she said, 'is they've no consideration.'

'No,' I said.

The Custodian

Susan Hill

AT FIVE MINUTES to three he climbed up the ladder into the loft. He went cautiously, he was always cautious now, moving his limbs warily, and never going out in bad weather without enough warm clothes. For the truth was that he had not expected to survive this winter, he was old, he had been ill for one week, and then the fear had come over him again, that he was going to die. He did not care for his own part, but what would become of the boy? It was only the boy he worried about now, only he who mattered. Therefore, he was careful with himself for he had lived out this bad winter, it was March, he could look forward to the spring and summer, could cease to worry for a little longer. All the same he had to be careful not to have accidents, though he was steady enough on his feet. He was seventy-one. He knew how easy it would be, for example, to miss his footing on the narrow ladder, to break a limb and lie there, while all the time the child waited, panic welling up inside him, left last at the school. And when the fear of his own dying did not grip him, he was haunted by ideas of some long illness, or incapacitation, and if he had to be taken into hospital, what would happen to the child, then? *What would happen?*

But now it was almost three o'clock, almost time for him to leave the house, his favourite part of the day, now he climbed on hands and knees into the dim, cool loft and felt about among the apples, holding this one and that one up to the beam of light coming through the slats in the roof, wanting the fruit he finally chose to be perfect, ripe and smooth.

The loft smelled sweetly of the apples and pears laid up there since the previous autumn. Above his head, he heard the scrabbling noises of the birds, house martins nesting in the eaves, his heart lurched with joy at the fresh realization that it was almost April, almost spring.

He went carefully down the ladder, holding the chosen apple. It took him twenty minutes to walk to the school but he liked to arrive early, to have the pleasure of watching and waiting, outside the gates.

The sky was brittle blue and the sun shone, but it was very cold, the air still smelled of winter. Until a fortnight ago there had been snow, he and the boy had trudged back and forwards every morning and afternoon over the frost-hard paths which led across the marshes, and the stream running alongside of them had been iced over, the reeds were stiff and white as blades.

It had thawed very gradually. Today, the air smelled thin and sharp in his nostrils. Nothing moved. As he climbed the grass bank onto the higher path, he looked across the great stretch of river, and it gleamed like a flat metal plate under the winter sun, still as the sky. Everything was pale, white and silver, a gull came over slowly and its belly and the undersides of its wings were pebbly grey. There were no sounds here except the sudden chatter of dunlin swooping and dropping quickly down, and the tread of his own feet on the path, the brush of his legs against grass clumps.

He had not expected to live this winter.

In his hand, he felt the apple, hard and soothing to the touch, for the boy must have fruit, fruit every day, he saw to that, as well as milk and eggs which they fetched from Maldrun at the farm, a mile away. His limbs should grow, he should be perfect.

Maldrun's cattle were out on their green island in the middle of the marshes, surrounded by the moat of steely water, he led them across a narrow path like a causeway, from the farm. They were like toy animals, or those in a picture seen from this distance away, they stood motionless, cut-out shapes of black and white. Every so often, the boy was still afraid of going past the island of cows, he gripped the old man's hand and a tight expression came over his face.

'They can't get at you, don't you see? They don't cross water, not cows. They're not bothered about you.'

'I know.'

And he did know – and was still afraid. Though there had been days, recently, when he would go right up to the edge of the strip of water, and stare across at the animals, he would even accompany Maldrun to the half-door of the milking parlour, and climb up and look over, would smell the thick, sour, cow-smell, and hear the splash of dung on to the stone floor. Then, he was not afraid. The cows had great, bony haunches and vacant eyes.

'Touch one,' Maldrun had said. The boy had gone inside and put out a hand, though standing well back, stretched and touched the rough pelt, and the cow had twitched, feeling the lightness of his hand as if it were an irritation, the prick of a fly. He was afraid, but getting less so, of the cows. So many things were changing, he was growing, he was seven years old.

Occasionally, the old man woke in the night and sweated with fear that he might die before the boy was grown, and he prayed, then, to live ten more years, just ten, until the boy could look after himself. And some days it seemed possible, seemed, indeed, most likely, some days he felt very young, felt no age at all, his arms were strong and he could chop wood and lift buckets, he was light-headed with the sense of his own youth. He was no age. He was seventy-one. A tall bony man with thick white hair, and without any spread of spare flesh. When he bathed, he looked down and saw every rib, every joint of his own thin body, he bent an arm and watched the flicker of muscle beneath the skin.

As the path curved round, the sun caught the surface of the water on his right, so that it shimmered and dazzled his eyes for a moment, and then he heard the familiar, faint, high moan of the wind, as it blew off the estuary a mile or more away. The reeds rustled dryly together like sticks. He put up the collar of his coat. But he was happy, his own happiness sang inside his head, that he was here, walking along this path with the apple inside his hand inside his pocket, that he would wait and watch and then, that he would walk back this same way with the boy, that none of those things he dreaded would come about.

Looking back, he could still make out the shapes of the cows, and looking down, to where the water lay between the reed-banks, he saw a swan, its neck arched and its head below the surface of the dark, glistening stream, and it too was entirely still. He stopped for a moment, watching it, and hearing the thin sound of the wind and then, turning, saw the whole, pale stretch of marsh and water and sky, saw for miles, back to where the trees began, behind which was the cottage and then far ahead, to where the sand stretched out like a tongue into the mouth of the estuary.

He was amazed, that he could be alive and moving, small as an insect across this great, bright, cold space, amazed that he should count for as much as Maldrun's cows and the unmoving swan.

The wind was suddenly cold on his face. It was a quarter past three. He left the path, went towards the gate, and began to cross the rough, ploughed field which led to the lane, and then, on another mile to the village, the school.

Occasionally, he came here not only in the morning, and back again in the afternoon, but at other times when he was overcome with sudden anxiety and a desire to see the boy, to reassure himself that he was still there, was alive. Then, he put down whatever he might be doing and came, almost running, stumbled and caught his breath, until he reached the railings and the closed, black gate. If he waited there long enough, if it was dinner or break time, he saw them all come streaming and tumbling out of the green painted doors, and he watched desperately until he saw him, and he could loosen the grip of his hands on the railings, the thumping of his heart eased, inside his chest. Always, then, the boy would come straight down to him, running over the asphalt, and laughed and called and pressed himself up against the railings on the other side.

'Hello.'

'All right are you?'

'What have you brought me? Have you got something?'

Though he knew there would be nothing, did not expect it, knew that there was only ever the fruit at home-time, apple, pear or sometimes, in the summer, cherries or a peach.

'I was just passing through the village.'

'Were you doing the shopping?'

'Yes. I only came up to see ...'

'We've done reading. We had tapioca for pudding.'

'That's good for you. You should eat that. Always eat your dinner.'

'Is it home-time yet?'

'Not yet.'

'You will be here won't you? You won't forget to come back?'

'Have I ever?'

Then, he made himself straighten his coat, or shift the string shopping bag over from one hand to the other, he said, 'You go back now then, go on to the others, you play with them,' for he knew that this was right, he should not keep the child standing here, should not show him up in front of the rest. It was only for himself that he had come, he was eaten up with his own concern, and fear.

'You go back to your friends now.'

'You will be here? You will be here?'

'I'll be here.'

He turned away, they both turned, for they were separate, they should have their own ways, their own lives. He turned and walked off down the lane out of sight of the playground, not allowing himself to look back, perhaps, he went and bought something from the shop, and he was calm again, no longer anxious, he walked back home slowly.

He did not mind all the walking, not even in the worst weather. He did not mind anything at all in this life he had chosen, and which was all-absorbing, the details of which were so important. He no longer thought anything of the past. Somewhere, he had read that an old man has only his memories, and he had wondered at that, for he had none, or rather, they did not concern him, they were like old letters which he had not troubled to keep. He had, simply, the present, the cottage, and the land around it, and the boy to look after. And he had to stay well, stay alive, he must not die yet. That was all.

But he did not often allow himself to go up to the school like that, at unnecessary times, he would force himself to stay and sweat out his anxiety and the need to reassure himself about the child, in some physical job, he would beat mats and plant vegetables in the garden, prune or pick from the fruit trees or walk over to see Maldrun at the farm, buy a chicken, and wait until the time came so slowly around to three o'clock, and he could go, with every reason, could allow himself the pleasure of arriving there a little early, and waiting beside the gates, which were now open, for the boy to come out.

'What have I got today?'

'You guess.'

'That's easy. Pear.'

'Wrong!' He opened his hand, revealing the apple.

'Well, I like apples best.'

'I know. I had a good look at those trees down the bottom this morning. There won't be so many this year. Mind, we've to wait for the blossom to be sure.'

'Last year there were hundreds of apples. *Thousands.*' He took the old man's hand as they reached the bottom of the lane. For some reason he always waited until just here, by the whitebeam tree, before doing so.

'There were *millions* of apples!'

'Get on!'

'Well, a lot anyway.'

'That's why there won't be so many this year. You don't get two crops like that in a row.'

'Why?'

'Trees wear themselves out, fruiting like that. They've to rest.'

'Will we have a lot of pears instead then?'

'I daresay. What have you done at school?'

'Lots of things.'

'Have you done your reading? That's what's the important thing. To keep up with your reading.'

He had started the boy off himself, bought alphabet and word picture books from the village, and, when they got beyond these, had made up his own, cut out pictures from magazines and written beside them in large clear letters on ruled sheets of paper. By the time the boy went to school, he had known more than any of the others, he was 'very forward', they had said, though looking him up and down at the same time for he was small for his age.

It worried him that the boy was still small, he watched the others closely as they came out of the gates and they were all taller, thicker in body and stronger of limb. His face was pale and curiously old looking beside theirs. He had always looked old.

The old man concerned himself even more, then, with the fresh eggs and cheese, milk and fruit, watched over the boy while he ate. But he did eat.

'We had meat and cabbage for dinner.'

'Did you finish it?'

'I had a second helping. Then we had cake for pudding. Cake and custard. I don't like that.'

'You didn't leave it?'

'Oh no. I just don't like it, that's all.'

Now, as they came on to the marshes, the water and sky were even paler and the reeds beside the stream were bleached, like old wood left out for years in the sun. The wind was stronger, whipping at their legs from behind.

'There's the swan.'

'They've a nest somewhere about.'

'Have you seen it?'

'They don't let you see it. They go away from it if anybody walks by.'

'I drew a picture of a swan.'

'Today?'

'No. Once. It wasn't very good.'

'If a thing's not good you should do it again.'

'Why should I?'

'You'll get better then.'

'I won't get better at drawing.' He spoke very deliberately, as he so often did, knowing himself, and firm about the truth of things, so that the old man was silent, respecting it.

'He's sharp,' Maldrun's wife said. 'He's a clever one.'

But the old man would not have him spoiled, or too lightly praised.

'He's plenty to learn. He's only a child yet.'

'All the same, he'll do, won't he? He's sharp.'

But perhaps it was only the words he used, only the serious expression on his face, which came of so much reading and all that time spent alone with the old man. And if he was, as they said, so sharp, so forward, perhaps it would do him no good?

He worried about that, wanting the boy to find his place easily in the world, he tried hard not to shield him from things, made him go to the farm to see Maldrun, and over Harper's fen by himself, to play with the gamekeeper's boys, told him always to mix with the others in the school playground, to do what they did. Because he was most afraid, at times, of their very contentment together, of the self-contained life they led, for in truth they needed no one, each of them would be entirely happy never to go far beyond this house: they spoke of all things, or of nothing, the boy read and made careful lists of the names of birds and moths, and built elaborate structures, houses and castles and palaces out of old matchboxes, he helped with the garden, had his own corner down beside the shed in which he grew what he chose. It had been like this from the beginning, from the day the old man had brought him here at nine months' old and set him down on the floor and taught him to crawl, they had fallen naturally into their life together. Nobody else had wanted him. Nobody else would have taken such care.

Once, people had been suspicious, they had spoken to each other in the village, had disapproved.

'He needs a woman there. It's not right. He needs someone who knows,' Maldrun's wife had said. But now, even she had accepted that it was not true, so that, before strangers, she would have defended them more fiercely than anyone.

'He's a fine boy, that. He's all right. You look at him, look. Well, you can't tell what works out for the best. You can never tell.'

By the time they came across the track which led between the gorse bushes and down through the fir trees, it was as cold as it had been on any night in January, they brought in more wood for the fire and had toast and the last of the damson jam and mugs of hot milk.

'It's like winter. Only not so dark. I like it in winter.'

But it was the middle of March now, in the marshes the herons and redshanks were nesting, and the larks spiralled up, singing through the silence. It was almost spring.

So, they went on as they had always done, until the second of April. Then, the day after their walk out to Derenow, the day after they saw the kingfisher, it happened.

From the early morning, he had felt uneasy, though there was no reason he could give for his fear, it simply lay, hard and cold as a stone in his belly, and he was restless about the house from the time he got up.

The weather had changed. It was warm and clammy, with low, dun-coloured clouds and, over the marshes, a thin mist. He felt the need to get out, to walk and walk, the cottage was dark and oddly quiet. When he went down between the fruit trees to the bottom of the garden the first of the buds were breaking into green but the grass was soaked with dew like a sweat, the heavy air smelled faintly rotten and sweet.

They set off in the early afternoon. The boy did not question, he was always happy to go anywhere at all but when he was asked to choose their route, he set off at once, a few paces ahead, on the path which forked away east, in the opposite direction from the village and leading, over almost three miles of empty marsh, towards the sea. They followed the bank of the river, and the water was sluggish, with fronds of dark green weed lying below the surface. The boy bent, and put his hand cautiously down, breaking the skin of the water, but when his fingers came up against the soft, fringed edges of the plants he pulled back.

'Slimey.'

'Yes. It's out of the current here. There's no freshness.'

'Will there be fish?'

'Maybe there will. Not so many.'

'I don't like it.' Though for some minutes he continued to peer between the reeds at the pebbles which were just visible on the bed of the stream. 'He asks questions,' they said. 'He takes an interest. It's his mind, isn't it – bright – you can see, alert, that's what. He's forever wanting to know.' Though there were times when he said nothing at all, his small, old-young face was crumpled in thought, there were times when he looked and listened with care and asked nothing.

'You could die here. You could drown in the water and never, never be found.'

'That's not a thing to think about. What do you worry over that for?'

'But you could, you could.'

They were walking in single file, the boy in front. From all the secret nests down in the reed beds, the birds made their own noises, chirring and whispering, or sending out sudden cries of warning and alarm. The high, sad call of a curlew came again and again, and then ceased abruptly. The boy whistled in imitation.

'Will it know it's me? Will it answer?'

He whistled again. They waited. Nothing. His face was shadowed with disappointment.

'You can't fool them, not birds.'

'You can make a blackbird answer you. You can easily.'

'Not the same.'

'Why isn't it?'

'Blackbirds are tame, blackbirds are garden birds.'

'Wouldn't a curlew come to the garden?'

'No.'

'Why wouldn't it?'

153

'It likes to be away from things. They keep to their own places.'

As they went on, the air around them seemed to close in further, it seemed harder to breathe, and they could not see clearly ahead to where the marshes and mist merged into the sky. Here and there, the stream led off into small, muddy pools and hollows, and the water in them was reddened by the rust seeping from some old can or metal crate thrown there and left for years, the stains which spread out looked like old blood. Gnats hovered in clusters over the water.

'Will we go onto the beach?'

'We could.'

'We might find something on the beach.'

Often, they searched among the pebbles for pieces of amber or jet, for old buckles and buttons and sea-smooth coins washed up by the tides, the boy had a collection of them in a cardboard box in his room.

They walked on, and then, out of the thick silence which was all around them came the creaking of wings, nearer and nearer and sounding like two thin boards of wood beaten slowly together. A swan, huge as an eagle, came over their heads, flying low, so that the boy looked up for a second in terror at the size and closeness of it, caught his breath. He said urgently, 'Swans go for people, swans can break your arm if they hit you, if they beat you with their wings. Can't they?'

'But they don't take any notice, so come on, you leave them be.'

'But they *can*, can't they?'

'Oh, they might.' He watched the great, grey-white shape go awkwardly away from them, in the direction of the sea.

A hundred yards further on, at the junction of two paths across the marsh, there was the ruin of a water mill, blackened after a fire years before, and half broken down, a sail torn off. Inside, under an arched doorway, it was dark and damp, the walls were coated with yellowish moss and water lay, brackish, in the mud hollows of the floor.

At high summer, on hot, shimmering blue days they had come across here on the way to the beach with a string bag full of food for their lunch, and then the water mill had seemed like a sanctuary, cool and silent, the boy had gone inside and stood there, had called softly and listened to the echo of his own voice as it rang lightly round and round the walls.

Now, he stopped dead in the path, some distance away.

'I don't want to go.'

'We're walking to the beach.'

'I don't want to go past that.'

'The mill?'

'There are rats.'

'No.'

'And flying things. Things that are black and hang upside down.'

'Bats? What's to be afraid of in bats? You've seen them, you've been in Maldrun's barn. They don't hurt.'

'I want to go back.'

'You don't have to go into the mill, who said you did? We're going on to where the sea is.'

'*I want to go back now.*'

He was not often frightened. But, standing there in the middle of the hushed stretch of fenland, the old man felt again disturbed himself, the fear that something would happen, here, where nothing moved and the birds lay hidden, only crying out their weird cries, where things lay under the unmoving water and the press of the air made him sweat down his back. Something would happen to them, something . . .

What could happen?

Then, not far ahead, they both saw him at the same moment, a man with a gun under his arm, tall and black and menacing as a crow against the dull horizon, and as they saw him, they also saw two mallard ducks rise in sudden panic from their nest in the reeds, and they heard the shots, three shots that cracked out and echoed for miles around, the air went on reverberating with the waves of terrible sound.

155

The ducks fell at once, hit in mid-flight so that they swerved, turned over, and plummeted down. The man with the shotgun started quickly forward and the grasses and reeds bent and stirred as a dog ran, burrowing, to retrieve. 'I want to go back, *I want to go back.*'

Without a word, the old man took his hand, and they turned, walked quickly back the way they had come, as though afraid that they, too, would be followed and struck down, not caring that they were out of breath and sticky with sweat, but only wanting to get away, to reach the shelter of the land and the trees, to make for home.

Nothing was ever said about it, or about the feeling they had both had walking across the marshes, the boy did not mention the man with the gun or the ducks which had been alive and in flight then so suddenly dead. All that evening, the old man watched him, as he stuck pictures in a book, and tore up dock leaves to feed the rabbit, watched for signs of left-over fear. But he was only, perhaps, quieter than usual, his face more closed up, he was concerned with his own thoughts.

In the night, he woke, and got up, went to the boy and looked down through the darkness, for fear that he might have had bad dreams and woken, but there was only the sound of his breathing, he lay quite still, very long and straight in the bed.

He imagined the future, and his mind was filled with images of all the possible horrors to come, the things which could cause the boy shock and pain and misery, and from which he would not be able to save him, as he had been powerless today to protect him from the sight of the killing of two ducks. He was in despair. Only the next morning, he was eased, as it came back to him again, the knowledge that he had, after all, lived out the winter and ahead of them lay only light and warmth and greenness.

Nevertheless, he half-expected that something would still happen to them, to break into their peace. For more than a week, nothing did, his fears were quieted, and then the spring broke, the apple and pear blossom weighed down the branches in great, creamy clots, the grass in the orchard grew up as high as the boy's knees, and across the marshes the sun shone and shone, the water of the river was turquoise, and in the streams, as clear as glass, the wind blew warm and smelled faintly of salt and earth. Walking to and from the school every day, they saw more woodlarks than they had ever seen, quivering on the air high above their heads, and near the gorse bushes, the boy found a nest of leverets. In the apple loft, the house martins hatched out and along the lanes, dandelions and buttercups shone golden out of the grass.

It was on the Friday that Maldrun gave the boy one of the farm kittens, and he carried it home close to his body beneath his coat. It was black and white like Maldrun's cows. And it was the day after that, the end of the first week of spring, that Blaydon came, Gilbert Blaydon, the boy's father.

He was sitting outside the door watching a buzzard hover above the fir copse when he heard the footsteps. He thought it was Maldrun bringing over the eggs, or a chicken – Maldrun generally came one evening in the week, after the boy had gone to bed, they drank a glass of beer and talked for half an hour. He was an easy man, undemonstrative. They still called one another, formally, 'Mr Bowry,' 'Mr Maldrun.'

The buzzard roved backwards and forwards over its chosen patch of air, searching.

When the old man looked down again, he was there, standing in the path. He was carrying a canvas kitbag.

He knew, then, why he had been feeling uneasy, he had expected this, or something like it, to happen, though he had put the fears to the back of his mind with the coming of sunshine and the leaf-breaking. He felt no hostility as he looked at Blaydon, only extreme weariness, almost as though he were ill.

There was no question of who it was, yet above all he ought to have expected a feeling of complete disbelief, for if anyone had asked, he would have said that he would certainly never see the boy's father again. But now he was here, it did not seem surprising, it seemed, indeed, somehow inevitable. Things had to alter, things could never go on. Happiness did not go on.

· 'Will you be stopping?'

Blaydon walked slowly forward, hesitated, and then set the kitbag down at his feet. He looked much older.

'I don't know if it'd be convenient.'

'There's a room. There's always a room.'

The old man's head buzzed suddenly in confusion, he thought he should offer a drink or a chair, should see to a bed, should ask questions to which he did not want to know the answers, should say something about the boy. *The boy.*

'You've come to take him . . ..'

Blaydon sat down on the other chair, beside the outdoors table. The boy looked like him, there was the same narrowness of forehead and chin, the same high-bridged nose. Only the mouth was different, though that might simply be because the boy's was still small and unformed.

'You've come to take him.'

'Where to?' He looked up. 'Where would I have, to take him to?'

But we don't want you here, the old man thought, we don't want anyone: and he felt the instrusion of this younger man, with the broad hands and long legs sprawled under the table, like a violent disturbance of the careful pattern of their lives, he was alien. *We don't want you.*

But what right had he to say that? He did not say it. He was standing up helplessly, not knowing what should come next, he felt the bewilderment as some kind of irritation inside his own head.

He felt old.

In the end, he managed to say, 'You'll not have eaten?'

Blaydon stared at him. 'Don't you want to know where I've come from?'

'No.'

'No.'

'I've made a stew. You'll be better for a plate of food.'

'Where is he?'

'Asleep in bed, where else would he be? I look after him, I know what I'm about. It's half past eight, gone, isn't it? What would he be doing but asleep in his bed, at half past eight?'

He heard his own voice rising and quickening, as he defended himself, defended both of them, he could prove it to this father or to anyone at all, how he'd looked after the boy. He would have said, what about you? Where have you been? What did you do for him? But he was too afraid, for he knew nothing about what rights Blaydon might have – even though he had never been near, never bothered.

'You could have been dead.'

'Did you think?'

'What was I to think? I knew nothing. Heard nothing.'

'No.'

Out of the corner of his eye, the old man saw the buzzard drop down suddenly, straight as a stone, on to some creature in the undergrowth of the copse. The sky was mulberry coloured and the honeysuckle smelled ingratiatingly sweet.

'I wasn't dead.'

The old man realized that Blaydon looked both tired and rather dirty, his nails were broken, he needed a shave and the wool at the neck of his blue sweater was unravelling. What was he to say to the boy then, when he had brought him up to be so clean and tidy and careful, had taken his clothes to be mended by a woman in the village, had always cut and washed his hair himself? What was he to tell him about this man?

'There's hot water. I'll get you linen, make you a bed. You'd best go up first, before I put out the stew. Have a wash.'

He went into the kitchen, took a mug and a bottle of beer and poured it out, and was calmed a little by the need to organize himself, by the simple physical activity.

When he took the beer out, Blaydon was still leaning back on the old chair. There were dark stains below his eyes.

'You'd best take it up with you.' The old man held out the beer.

159

It was almost dark now. After a long time, Blaydon reached out, took the mug and drank, emptying it in four or five long swallows, and then, as though all his muscles were stiff, rose slowly, took up the kitbag, went towards the house.

When the old man had set the table and dished out the food, he was trembling. He tried to turn his mind away from the one thought. That Blaydon had come to take the boy away.

He called and when there was no reply, went up the stairs. Blaydon was stretched out on his belly on top of the unmade bed, heavy and motionless in sleep.

While he slept, the old man worried about the morning. It was Saturday, there would not be the diversion of going to school, the boy must wake and come downstairs and confront Blaydon.

What he had originally said, was, your mother died, your father went away. And that was the truth. But he doubted if the boy so much as remembered; he had asked a question only once, and that more than two years ago.

They were content together, needing no one.

He sat on the straight-back chair in the darkness, surrounded by hidden greenery and the fumes of honeysuckle, and tried to imagine what he might say.

'This is your father. Other boys have fathers. This is your father who came back, who will stay with us here. For some time, or perhaps not for more than a few days. His name is Gilbert Blaydon.

'Will you call him 'father'?, will you . . .

'This is . . .'

His mind broke down before the sheer cliff confronting it and he simply sat on, hands uselessly in front of him on the outdoors table, he thought of nothing, and on white plates in the kitchen the stew cooled and congealed and the new kitten from Maldrun's farm slept, coiled on an old green jumper. The cat, the boy, the boy's father, all slept. From the copse, the throaty call of the night-jars.

'You'll be ready for breakfast. You didn't eat the meal last night.'

'I slept.'

'You'll be hungry.' He had his back to Blaydon. He was busy with the frying pan and plates over the stove. What had made him tired enough to sleep like that, from early evening until now, fully clothed on top of the bed! But he didn't want to know, would not ask questions.

The back door was open on to the path that led down between vegetable beds and the bean canes and currant bushes, towards the thicket. Blaydon went to the doorway.

'Two eggs, will you have?'

'If . . .'

'There's plenty.' He wanted to divert him, talk to him, he had to pave the way. The boy was there, somewhere at the bottom of the garden.

'We'd a hard winter.'

'Oh, yes?'

'Knee deep, all January, all February, we'd to dig ourselves out of the door. And then it froze – the fens froze right over, ice as thick as your fist. I've never known like it.'

But now it was spring, now outside there was the bright, glorious green of new grass, new leaves, now the sun shone.

He began to set out knives and forks on the kitchen table. It would have to come, he would have to call the boy in, to bring them together. What would he say? His heart squeezed and then pumped hard, suddenly, in the thin bone-cage of his chest.

Blaydon's clothes were creased and crumpled. And they were not clean. Had he washed himself? The old man tried to get a glimpse of his hands.

'I thought I'd get a job,' Blaydon said.

The old man watched him.

'I thought I'd look for work.'

'Here?'

'Around here. Is there work?'

'Maybe. I've not had reason to find out. Maybe.'

'If I'm staying on, I'll need to work.'

'Yes.'

'It'd be a help, I daresay?'

'You've a right to do as you think fit. You make up your own mind.'

'I'll pay my way.'

'You've no need to worry about the boy, if it's that. He's all right, he's provided for. You've no need to find money for him.'

'All the same . . .'

After a minute, Blaydon walked over and sat down at the table.

The old man thought, he is young, young and strong and fit, he has come here to stay, he has every right, he's the father. He is . . .

But he did not want Blaydon in their lives, did not want the hands resting on the kitchen table, and the big feet beneath it.

He said, 'You could try at the farm. At Maldrun's. They've maybe got work there. You could try.'

'Maldrun's farm?'

'It'd be ordinary work. Labouring work.'

'I'm not choosy.'

The old man put out eggs and fried bread and bacon onto the plates, poured tea, filled the sugar basin. And then he had no more left to do, he had to call the boy.

But nothing happened as he had feared it, after all.

He came in. 'Wash your hands.' But he was already half way to the sink, he had been brought up so carefully, the order was not an order but a formula between them, regular, and of comfort.

'Wash your hands.'

'I've come to stay,' Blaydon said at once, 'for a bit. I got here last night.'

The boy hesitated in the middle of the kitchen, looked from one to the other of them, trying to assess this sudden change in the order of things.

'For a week or two,' the old man said. 'Eat your food.'

The boy got on to his chair. 'What's your name?'

'Gilbert Blaydon.'

'What have I to call you?'

'Either.'

'Gilbert, then.'

'What you like.'

After that, they got on with eating; the old man chewed his bread very slowly, filled, for the moment, with relief.

Maldrun took him on at the farm as a general labourer and then their lives formed a new pattern, with the full upsurge of spring. Blaydon got up, and ate his breakfast with them and then left, there was a quarter of an hour which the old man had alone with the boy before setting off across the marsh path to school, and in the afternoon, an even longer time. Blaydon did not return, sometimes, until after six.

At the weekend, he went off somewhere alone, but occasionally, he took the boy for walks; they saw the heron's nest, and then the cygnets, and once, a peregrine, flying over the estuary. The two of them were at ease together.

Alone, the old man tried to imagine what they might be saying to each other, he walked distractedly about the house, and almost wept, with anxiety and dread. They came down the path, and the boy was sitting up on Blaydon's shoulders, laughing and laughing.

'You've told him.'

Blaydon turned, surprised, and then sent the boy away. 'I've said nothing.'

The old man believed him. But there was still a fear for the future, the end of things.

The days lengthened. Easter went by, and the school holidays, during which the old man was happiest, because he had so much time with the boy to himself, and then it was May, in the early mornings there was a fine mist above the blossom trees.

'He's a good worker,' Maldrun said, coming over one evening with the eggs and finding the old man alone. 'I'm glad to have him.'

'Yes.'

'He takes a bit off your shoulders, I daresay.'

'He pays his way.'

'No. Work, I meant. Work and worries. All that.'

What did Maldrun know? But he only looked back at the old man, his face open and friendly, drank his bottled beer.

He thought about it, and realised that it was true. He had grown used to having Blaydon about, to carry the heavy things and lock up at night, to clear out the fruit loft and lop off the overhanging branches and brambles at the entrance to the thicket. He had slipped into their life, and established himself. When he thought of the future without Blaydon, it was to worry. For the summer was always short and then came the run down through autumn into winter again. Into snow and ice and cold, and the north-east wind scything across the marshes. He dreaded all that, now that he was old. Last winter, he had been ill once, and for only a short time. This winter he was a year older, anything might happen. He thought of the mornings when he would have to take the boy to school before it was even light, thought of the frailty of his own flesh, the brittleness of his bones, he looked in the mirror at his own weak and rheumy eyes.

He had begun to count on Blaydon's being here to ease things, to help with the coal and wood and the breaking of ice on pails, to be in some way an insurance against his own possible illness, possible death.

Though now, it was still only the beginning of summer, now, he watched Blaydon build a rabbit hutch for the boy, hammering nails and sawing wood, uncoiling wire skilfully. He heard them laugh suddenly together. This was what he needed, after all, not a woman about the place, but a man, the strength and ease of a man who was not old, did not fear, did not say, 'Wash your hands', 'Drink up all your milk', 'Take care.'

The kitten grew, and spun about in quick, mad circles in the sun.

'He's a good worker,' Maldrun said.

After a while, the old man took to dozing in his chair outside, after supper, while Blaydon washed up, emptied the bins and then took out the shears, to clip the hedge or the grass borders, when the boy had gone to bed.

But everything that had to do with the boy, the business of rising and eating, going to school and returning, the routine of clothes and food and drink and bed, all that was still supervised by the old man. Blaydon did not interfere, scarcely seem to notice what was done. His own part in the boy's life was quite different.

In June and early July, it was hotter than the old man could ever remember. The gnats droned in soft, grey clouds under the trees, and over the water of the marshes. The sun shone hard and bright and still the light played tricks so that the estuary seemed now very near, now very far away. Maldrun's cows tossed their heads, against the flies which gathered stickily in the runnels below their great eyes.

He began to rely more and more upon Blaydon as the summer reached its height, left more jobs for him to do, because he was willing and strong, and because the old man succumbed easily to the temptation to rest himself in the sun. He still did most of the cooking but he would let Blaydon go down to the shops and the boy often went with him. He was growing, his limbs were filling out and his skin was berry-brown. He lost the last of the pink-and-whiteness of babyhood. He had accepted Blaydon's presence without question and was entirely used to him, though he did not show any less affection for the old man, who continued to take care of him day by day. But he became less nervous and hesitant, more self-assured, he spoke of things in a casual, confident voice, learned much from his talks with Blaydon. He still did not know that this was his father. The old man thought there was no reason to tell him – not yet, not yet, they could go on as they were for the time being, just as they were.

He was comforted by the warmth of the sun on his face, by the scent of the roses and the tobacco plants in the evening, the sight of the scarlet bean-flowers clambering higher and higher up their frame.

He had decided right at the beginning that he himself would ask no questions of Blaydon, would wait until he should be told. But he was not told. Blaydon's life might have begun only on the day he had arrived here. The old man wondered if he had been in prison, or else abroad, working on a ship, though he had no evidence for either. In the evenings they drank beer together and occasionally played a game of cards, though more often, Blaydon worked at something in the garden and the old man simply sat, watching him, hearing the last cries of the birds from the marshes.

With the money Blaydon brought in, they bought new clothes for the boy, and better cuts of meat, and then, one afternoon, a television set arrived with two men in a green van to erect the aerial.

'For the winter,' Blaydon said. 'Maybe you won't bother with it now. But it's company in the winter.'

'I've never felt the lack.'

'All the same.'

'I don't need entertainment. We make our own. Always have made our own.'

'You'll be glad of it once you've got the taste. I told you – it's for the winter.'

But the old man watched it sometimes very late in the evenings of August and discovered things of interest to him, new horizons were opened, new worlds.

'I'd not have known that,' he said. 'I've never travelled. Look at what I'd never have known.'

Blaydon nodded. He himself seemed little interested in the television set. He was mending the front fence, staking it all along with old wood given him by Maldrun at the farm. Now, the gate would fit closely and not swing and bang in the gales of winter.

It was on a Thursday night towards the end of August that Blaydon mentioned the visit to the seaside.

'He's never been,' he said, wiping the foam of beer from his top lip. 'He told me. I asked him. He's never been to the sea.'

'I've done all I can. There's never been the money. We've managed as best we could.'

'You're not being blamed.'

'I'd have taken him, I'd have seen to it in time. Sooner or later.'

'Yes.'

'Yes.'

'Well – I could take him.'

'To the sea?'

'To the coast, yes.'

'For a day? It's far enough.'

'A couple of days, I thought. For a weekend.'

The old man was silent. But it was true. The boy had never been anywhere and perhaps he suffered because of it, perhaps at school the others talked of where they had gone, what they had seen, shaming him; if that was so, he should be taken, should go everywhere, he must not miss anything, must not be left out.

'Just a couple of days. We'd leave first thing Saturday morning and come back Monday. I'd take a day off.'

He had been here three months now, and not missed a day off work.

'You do as you think best.'

'I'd not go without asking you.'

'It's only right. He's at the age for taking things in. He needs enjoyment.'

'Yes.'

'You go. It's only right.'

'I haven't told him, not yet.'

'You tell him.'

When he did, the boy's face opened out with pleasure, he licked his lips nervously over and over again in his excitement, already counting until it should be time to go. The old man went upstairs and sorted out clothes for him, washed them carefully and hung them on the line, he began himself to anticipate it all. This was right. The boy should go.

But he dreaded it. They had not been separated before. He could not imagine how it would be, to sleep alone in the cottage, and then he began to imagine all the possible accidents. Blaydon had not asked him if he wanted to go with them. But he did not. He felt suddenly too tired to leave the house, too tired for any journeys or strangers, he wanted to sit on his chair in the sun and count the time until they should be back.

He had got used to the idea of Blaydon's continuing presence here, he no longer lived in dread of the coming winter. It seemed a long time since the days when he had been alone with the boy.

They set off very early on the Saturday morning, before the sun had broken through the thick mist that hung low over the marshes. Every sound was clear and separate as it came through the air, he heard their footsteps, the brush of their legs against the grasses long after they were out of sight. The boy had his own bag, bought new in the village, a canvas bag strapped across his shoulders. He had stood up very straight, eyes glistening, already his mind was filled with imaginary pictures of what he would see, what they would do.

The old man went back into the kitchen and put the kettle on again, refilled the teapot for himself and planned what he was going to do. He would work, he would clean out all the bedrooms of the house and sort the boy's clothes for any that needed mending; he would polish the knives and forks and wash the curtains and walk down to the village for groceries, he would bake a cake and pies, prepare a stew, ready for their return.

So that, on the first day, the Saturday, he scarcely had time to think of them, to notice their absence and in the evening, his legs and back ached, he sat for only a short time outside, after his meal, drunk with tiredness, and slept later than usual on the Sunday morning.

It was then that he felt the silence and emptiness of the house. He walked about it uselessly, he woke up the kitten and teased it with a feather so that it would play with him, distract his attention from his own solitude. When it slept again, he went out, and walked for miles across the still, hot marshes. The water between the reed beds was very low and even dried up altogether in places revealing the dark, greenish-brown slime below. The faint, dry whistling sound that usually came through the rushes was absent. He felt parched as the countryside after this long, long summer, the sweat ran down his bent back.

He had walked in order to tire himself out again but this night he slept badly and woke out of clinging nightmares with a thudding heart, tossed from side to side, uncomfortable among the bedclothes. But tomorrow he could begin to count the strokes of the clock until their return.

He got up feeling as if he had never slept, his eyes were pouched and blurred. But he began the baking, the careful preparations to welcome them home. He scarcely stopped for food himself all day, though his head and his back ached, he moved stiffly about the kitchen.

When they had not returned by midnight on the Monday, he did not go down to the village, or across to Maldrun's farm to telephone the police and the hospitals. He did nothing. He knew.

But he sat up in the chair outside the back door all night with the silence pressing in on his ears. Once or twice his head nodded down on to his chest, he almost slept, but then jerked awake again, shifted a little, and sat on in the darkness.

He thought, they have not taken everything, some clothes are left, clothes and toys and books, they must mean to come back. But he knew that they did not. Other toys, other clothes, could be bought anywhere.

A week passed and the summer slid imperceptibly into

autumn. Like smooth cards shuffled together in a pack, the trees faded to yellow and crinkled at the edges.

He did not leave the house, and he ate almost nothing, only filled and refilled the teapot, and drank.

He did not blame Gilbert Blaydon, he blamed himself for having thought to keep the boy, having planned out their whole future. When the father had turned up, he should have known what he wanted at once, should have said, 'Take him away, take him now,' to save them this furtiveness, this deception. At night, though, he worried most about the effect it would have on the boy, who had been brought up so scrupulously, to be tidy and clean, to eat up his food, to learn. He wished there was an address to which he could write a list of details about the boy's everyday life, the routine he was used to following.

He waited for a letter. None came. The pear trees sagged under their weight of ripe, dark fruit and after a time it fell with soft thuds into the long grass. He did not gather it up and take it to store in the loft, he left it there for the sweet pulp to be burrowed by hornets and grubs. But sometimes he took a pear and ate it himself, for he had always disapproved of waste.

He kept the boy's room exactly as it should be. His clothes were laid out neatly in the drawers, his books lined on the single shelf, in case he should return. But he could not bother with the rest of the house, dirt began to linger in corners. Fluff accumulated greyly beneath beds. The damp patch on the bathroom wall was grown over with moss like a fungus when the first rain came in October.

Maldrun had twice been across from the farm and received no answer to his questions. In the village, the women talked. October went out in fog and drizzle, and the next time Maldrun came the old man did not open the door. Maldrun waited, peering through the windows between cupped hands, and in the end left the eggs on the back step.

The old man got up later and later each day, and went to bed earlier, to sleep between the frowsty, unwashed sheets. For a short while he turned on the television set in the evenings and sat staring at whatever was offered to him, but in the end he did not bother, only stayed in the kitchen while it grew dark around him. Outside, the last of the fruit fell onto the sodden garden and lay there untouched. Winter came.

In the small town flat, Blaydon set out plates, cut bread and opened tins, filled the saucepan with milk.

'Wash your hands,' he said. But the boy was already there, moving his hands over and over the pink soap, obediently, wondering what was for tea.

Notes

The notes in this edition are intended to serve the needs of overseas students as well as those of British-born users.

The Patriot Son

2 *gable-end:* part of house where walls slope under roof.

Gaelic: Irish.

haberdashery: sewing-aids counter.

traps: horse-drawn carts.

R.I.C.: Royal Irish Constabulary (now the Royal Ulster Constabulary), the traditional enemy of the Irish Republican Army since 1919.

ledgers swelling with debt: account books growing fat only with records of money customers owe the shopkeeper.

3 *Fenian:* member of secret nineteenth-century organization which fought against British rule in Ireland.

drilling: doing military training.

4 *Walls of Limerick ... Bridge of Athlone:* Irish formation folk dances.

be in the swim of things: know what is going on.

face: courage.

incredulous: disbelieving.

contemptuous: scornful.

eejits: idiots (the spelling conveys the Irish pronunciation of the word).

fancy: imagine.

5 *shutters were put up:* window protectors were in place (i.e. to show the shop was shut).

undercurrent of intrigue: hidden plot.

There are no flies on you: (slang) You are not easily fooled.

affably: in a pleasantly relaxed way.

pronounced discretion: obvious secrecy.

The Colleen Bawn: The Fair Child, a murder play by Dion Boucicault.

doctored: altered (to give a revolutionary meaning).

sheep ... goats: the innocent and the guilty.

have: (slang) confuse.

6 *baleful:* threatening.

cracked: crazy.

baize: felt-like woollen cloth for covering games tables and doors.

7 *inconsequentially:* for no apparent reason.

as she read it: Matty's mother seems to understand Gaelic.

8 *freakishly:* suddenly.

10 *the Movement:* organization attempting to free Northern Ireland from Britain.

grille: grating, bars on the window of a prison door.

11 *in dejection:* feeling depressed and sad.

volley of oaths: rapid burst of swear words.

12 *cranky:* bad-tempered.

ostentatiously: in an obvious way.

compliment: favour.

lobby: hallway, corridor, passage.

13 *reminiscences:* memories.

under a compliment to him: owing him a favour.

14 *cryptic:* mysterious.

preposterous: ridiculously unlikely.

on the uptake: to understand.

appalled: horrified.

15 *implication:* suggestion.

belittling in the concession: insulting in being allowed (to escape from danger).

16 *malicious:* intentionally criminal.

17 *civilian:* not in uniform, non-fighting.

sundered: parted.

veered: changed direction.

enormity: evil wickedness.

18 *acrid:* unpleasantly bitter.

lurched: staggered.

rasped: said in a grating, scratchy voice.

bunny: little rabbit.

19 *patriot:* fighter for your country's freedom.

abortive: unsuccessful.

stupefaction: astonishment.

20 *constabulary:* policemen.

agile: quick-moving.

elation: pride.

that had eluded him: that he had been trying to find.

intoxication: drunkenness.

21 *lacerated:* ripped.

fang: long tooth.

wheedling: coaxing, persuading (the police that she is telling the truth).

gom!: fool!

Country Lovers

koppies: small hills on the veld.

mealie lands: maize fields.

veld: South African grassland with some shrubs and trees.

kraal: tribal village.

spans: yokes.

platteland: backveld, remote or backward area.

25 *leguaan:* iguana, tree-lizard with crest along its back.

stinkwood: unpleasant smelling relative of laurel.

Cape willow: South African catkin tree.

eroded: worn away.

26 *Blanco:* protective treatment for belts and harness fabrics, mostly white and used in the army.

dividing them: telling them it was time to go.

28 *floss:* silky fibre.

matt: unshiny.

opaque: not transparent, muddy.

29 *gilded:* gold-coloured.
  grimace: twisted expression.
31 *pathological:* medical abnormality.
  intestinal: below the stomach.
  perjury: lying under oath in a court of law.

The Heart

34 *Hari:* name for the Hindu god Vishnu, the Preserver.
  strip: take off his outer clothes.
  fancifully: elaborately, with more imagination than accuracy.
  advised against over-exertion: warned that he should not try to do too much.
  fly-leaf: first (blank) page.
  tuck shop: school sweet shop.
  Alsatians: large, intelligent, wolf-like dogs, used as guards and for police work.
  veranda: porch along sides and front of house.
35 *in relay:* continuously, by taking turns.
  aggravated their fury: made their anger worse.
  bolted: darted away.
  misgivings: fearful doubts.
36 *lot:* land enclosed (by wire fence).
  esteem: popularity and respect.
  asphalt: smooth brownish-black road surface.
  trolley-buses: electric buses which draw their power from a wheel (trolley) running along a double overhead cable.
37 *trolley-poles sparking blue:* swinging rod connects the top of the bus to the trolley, which gives off electric sparks as it turns.
  exertion: effort.
38 *languor:* lack of interest.
  Lassie Come Home: the first film about the sheepdog Lassie, made in America in 1943, starring Elizabeth Taylor.

39 *recognition:* appreciation, thanks, friendliness.

saliva: spittle.

binding the skin: curing the cut. Saliva has antiseptic and healing properties.

40 *anthurium lilies:* tropical evergreen South American relatives of the European Arum lily, with bitter juice and ugly smell.

cornered: trapped.

trellis: support frame.

Bleeding Heart vine: climbing plant with red heart-shaped flowers.

'I have no appetite': Hari's desire for food has been satisfied by torturing his puppy; his father has spent his lunch time upstairs with his mother.

41 *he could punish only when his parents were away or occupied:* Hari knows his parents would object to his treatment of the puppy.

complementary: equal and opposite.

42 *'He ran out just as your father was driving in':* the dog is no longer permanently chained, and is now too big for Hari's mother to 'Hold him!'

The Second Hut

44 *not to deviate further than snapping point from:* just managing to keep to the 'normal life' (*deviate:* turn aside, *snapping:* breaking).

inclinations: desires.

unconforming: refusing to join in.

close-bitten: tight-lipped.

khaki: dust-coloured.

going to seed: losing his energy like an untended plant.

shack: rough hut.

seedy: decaying and shabby.

45 *stoicism:* endurance. The Stoic philosophers of ancient

Rome practised self-control, showing neither pleasure nor pain.

penetrate: make any impression on.

solicitude: concern.

scrupulous: conscientious.

46 *strained:* tired.

intolerable strain: unbearable burden.

commodity: profitable item.

incredulously: disbelievingly.

ironically: mockingly.

slack: loose.

failure of will: lack of determination.

slops: liquid food for invalids.

47 *native bearer:* African messenger.

sparsely: thinly.

veranda: long porch.

prey: victim.

the essence of: perfect.

48 *obtuse:* blunt.

Afrikander: South African descended from the Dutch farmer settlers (Boers).

Boer War: fighting over land in South Africa between British and Dutch in 1881 and 1899–1901.

scrupulously: honestly.

49 *the bush:* uncultivated land with shrubs and trees.

dung: animal manure.

musty: mouldy.

felted: matted.

butcher-bird: shrike, which kills small birds and insects by spiking them on thorns.

cache: hidden store.

50 *laconic:* short, brief.

ignorant of technicalities: knowing nothing about details.

passage money: boat fare.

resentment: anger at sense of injustice.

galled: annoyed and humiliated.

propitiating fate: keeping friendly with the gods.

irrational: absurd and strange, unreasonable.

51 *flaxen:* pale yellow. (Flax is a plant fibre.)

tow: broken flax.

sapless: lifeless.

hide: animal skin.

squalor: dirt and poverty.

52 *maize:* Indian corn, of which sweetcorn is a variety.

scything: slicing with curved blades.

foetid: stinking.

moorless: anchorless, adrift.

preliminaries: politely leading up to it.

53 *incessant:* non-stop.

mealie meal: maize flour. See note to page 24 on *mealie lands.*

54 *brusquely:* abruptly and with apparent rudeness.

stocky: short and sturdily well-built.

bossboy: head native labourer.

55 *oppressors:* harsh rulers.

kraals: see note to page 24 on *kraal.*

kept this side of: just avoided.

passive resistance: enmity shown by non-violent non-cooperation.

repugnant: very disagreeable.

assented: agreed.

56 *diffident:* shy.

ruefully: pretending sorrow.

querulous: complaining peevishly.

involuntarily: unintentionally.

58 *baas:* boss, master.

antagonism: opposition.

compound: fenced-in group of huts for native workers.

disproportionate: greater than reasonable.

malignant: evil-wishing.

exuberance: high spirits.

elemental: basic.

irrepressible: uncontrollable.

fecundity: fertility.

irresistible: unstoppable.

59 *repulsive:* disgusting.

implied: suggested.

kernels: inside of nuts.

60 *scamp the work:* work carelessly and hastily.

61 *superseded:* made to feel inferior.

perfunctorily: with the least possible effort.

premonitions: sense of trouble to come.

62 *raillery:* teasing.

63 *pungent:* pricking the eyes and nose.

veld: open country in South Africa.

64 *incandescently:* glowing from within.

The Boss

70 *reprovingly:* accusingly, scoldingly.

71 *'It's a long time she's been here':* typically Jewish inversion of 'She's been here a long time'.

72 *You won't be:* similarly, 'Won't you be'.

querulous: complaining.

shrugging movements: Jewish characteristic.

paternal regard: father-like concern.

73 *all the white employees:* the black workers would automatically show respect, even to a small boy.

presumed on: took advantage of.

presumption: assumption (that being Jewish made her his equal).

wheedled: coaxed, flattered.

74 *consolation:* comfort for having lost.

75 *brusquely:* hurriedly, almost rudely.

wary: watchful, cautious.

When will that be? ... Say the bells of Stepney: lines from the children's nursery rhyme 'Oranges and Lemons'.

Raspberry Jam

84 *prim:* over-polite.

indelible: cannot be removed.

patronizing: condescendingly superior.

lapse: sink, slip.

feigned abstraction: pretended absent-mindedness.

freaks: abnormal, strange or odd specimens.

85 *enamel:* glossy paint (make-up or nail varnish).

Don Bradman: Australian cricketer, often scoring over 200 runs an innings; one of the highest-scoring batsmen ever.

Gordon Richards: English champion jockey 26 times from 1920 to 1954.

a bee in her bonnet: crazy obsession.

Bolsheviks: Russian communists, or revolutionaries.

'un: one.

86 *consign:* send.

bouts: spells or fits (of drinking).

livid: purplish grey-blue (like a bruise) with anger.

squalid: dirty (scandalous).

take the floor: speak in the debate.

relinquish it: give it (the position of speaker) up.

loquacity: talkativeness.

exagéré: (*French*) exaggerated.

solaces: ways of comforting herself (with drink).

87 *wistful:* sadly wishing or longing.

Conder: Charles (1868–1909), painted beautiful fans in water colour on silk.

Whistler: American nineteenth-century painter, famous for his 'Portrait of My Mother', who settled in Chelsea and greatly influenced all he met.

Rossetti: Dante Gabriel (1828–1882), famous as a poet as well as a painter.

patina: green crust on old bronze, and also the glossy surface produced by age on silver and wood.

been away: been put away.

outmoded: out of fashion.

asylum: mental home.

ken: range of knowledge.

88 *inhibitions:* psychological inabilities.

phobias: exaggerated fears.

morbid: sickly, or gruesome.

libido: person's life-energy and sexual drive.

jitterbugging: jazz dancing.

solicitous: anxious.

89 *stratagem:* deceitful scheme.

restrained: held back, stopped.

Grimm: the Grimm brothers' collection of German fairy-tales.

Arabian Nights: the *Thousand and One Nights* collection of Eastern tales.

Alice's adventures: recounted in the books *Alice in Wonderland* and *Alice Through the Looking Glass* by Lewis Carroll.

90 *bridge:* card game for two couples.

'vulnerable': liable to lose points in a game of Contract Bridge. Normally 'vulnerable' means weak or helpless. Johnnie thinks they mean the same thing.

Lydia Bennet: character in Jane Austen's novel *Pride and Prejudice*.

'got tight': drunk.

Hunt Ball: dinner dance for members of the local fox hunt.

'co-respondent': the person with whom the guilty marriage-partner is unfaithful. 'Correspondent' shoes match or go with your outfit. Johnnie thinks they are the same word, never having seen them written.

Little Dorrit: novel by Charles Dickens.

'leg cuts and fine shots to cover': ways of batting in cricket.

grand vizier: prime minister of the old Turkish Empire, a frequent character in the *Arabian Nights* stories.

Red Queen: character in *Alice Through the Looking Glass*.

flayed: skinned.

91 *cissie:* effeminate or girlish man.

irrevocable: unchangeable.

Queen Alexandra: (1844–1925), wife of Edward VII.

Brighton Pavilion: built in 1782 as a centre for lavish entertainment.

Caro: (*Italian*) 'dear'.

brusque: abrupt, almost rude.

92 *bluff:* honestly plain-speaking.

Crown Prince: title given to the heir to the throne of a foreign country.

anecdotes: short stories about particular incidents.

rum: (slang) peculiar or strange.

self-conscious whimsicality: embarrassed playfulness, or pretending to be eccentric or imaginative for effect.

magpie propensity: tendency to hoard things at random, as magpies (black and white crows) do.

workhouses: places where very poor people used to be housed.

slandering: damaging with lies.

whispering campaign: organized circulation of wicked rumours.

93 *instantaneous:* immediate.

Johnnie head in the air: 'Little Johnny Head-in-Air' is one of Heinrich Hoffman's *Struwwelpeter* verses. They are all warning of dreadful things that happen to naughty children.

impulsively: enthusiastically.

precocity: early maturity.

94 *depredations:* stealing and damage.

big pots: (slang) important people.

'soppy': silly, sentimental.

mazurka: lively Polish dance with strong 3/4 beat, usually played loudly.

95 *drinking:* drinking alcohol.

precarious: dangerously uncertain.

accommodate: reconcile or fit.

benefactress: lady giving the money.

take a back seat: watch without taking part.

96 *dictate:* give orders.

innuendos: sly hints.

veiledly coarse: disguisedly crude.

libel: writing a false accusation. Miss Marian is confusing it with slander, which is spoken.

conquest: man attracted to her.

Southdown: bus company operating in the Brighton area.

jalouse: (*French*) jealous.

épris: (*French*) in love.

97 *vexed:* annoyed.

play ball: join in the game.

vermilion: the brilliant red of mercuric sulphide.

audacious: daringly bold.

leering pruriently: glancing slyly and sexily.

Johnny Weismuller: American Olympic athlete who played Tarzan and Jungle Jim in films until the 1950s.

spasms: fits.

98 *maudlin:* drunkenly weeping.

debauch: bout of excessive indulgence (in drink).

malignity: evil intention.

99 *sojourn:* stay.

espouse: join with, support.

charmeuse: soft, smooth, silk fabric.

Asti: North Italian town near Milan.

E come era bello, caro Gabriele: (*Italian*) and how handsome he was, dear Gabriel.

arte dell' amore: (*Italian*) art of love.

100 *lire:* small Italian coins which Miss Dolly paid the donkey boy to dance with her.

parody: mocking imitation.

tanto cattivo: (*Italian*) so wicked.

spasmodically: fitfully, jerkily.

The Saint

104 *investor:* share-buyer.

sect: religious group.

capital: money.

found ourselves: discovered that we were.

dragged into the courts: forced to defend ourselves against legal action.

consumption: tuberculosis.

exhilarating: gladdening, cheering.

vulgar: common ordinary people.

irritability: impatience, annoyance.

105 *impudence:* impertinence, cheek, nerve.

conundrum: word riddle.

casuistry: method of false logic.

scored: permanently marked with lines.

abrupt: hasty.

dogmas: systems of belief.

jargon: special language.

trade terms: professional expressions.

pince-nez: spectacles which clip onto the nose.

106 *punts:* long flat boats.

reach: straight section of river.

eminent: notable, famous.

with proper reserve: not openly of course.

chamois: soft antelope skin.

107 *torpid:* numb, barely moving.

enamelled: smooth, hard-painted, artificial.

decontaminated: disinfected.

108 *incredulous:* disbelieving.

blazers: striped sports jackets.

flannels: sports trousers.

109 *insignificant:* unimportant.

material: worldly, unspiritual.

chloride: yellowy-green chemical, like chlorine.

launches: motorized pleasure boats.

110 *pennants:* small pointed flags.
   well: area in a punt behind the seats. In Oxford this is where the punter stands.
   stern: back of boat.
   eddies: swirls of water.
   Deferentially: out of respect for him.
111 *irritation:* nuisance.
   lunged: pushed suddenly.
   damson: small plum.
112 *unperturbed and genteel:* unruffled and civilized.
   Euclid: famous Greek-Egyptian mathematician of the third century BC.
113 *pant-loops:* tapes to tie shirt to underpants.
   brace-tabs: flaps to attach shirt to braces.
   The waist of Mr Timberlake's shirt is well-supplied with small attachments to stop his shirt riding up or his braces twisting round, to keep him looking smart. Under strain, however, they are too tight and cause the shirt to split.
   monumental: great and permanent.
   mortal: able to die, human.
   had come to nobody: had not been made to anyone.
   amputated: cut off.
   torso ... bust ... head and shoulders: these are technical terms used in sculpture. (*torso:* legless body; *bust:* upper quarter of human body.)
   deprecation: mild disapproval.
   pathos: sadness.
   platter: large plate.
114 *blasphemed:* spoken irreligiously.
   bolster: long, large pillow.
   glaze: hard, glossy coating.
   sedentary: used to sitting down.
115 *indulgence:* pleasure.
   flaccid: loosely wrinkled, limp.
   inert: unmoving.
   preoccupied: lost in thought.

immaterial habitation: spiritual home. 'Immaterial' also means 'unimportant'.

deposit: mud, sediment.

effervescence: gas bubbles, fizz.

metaphysical: abstract or supernatural.

pettish: sulky, annoyed.

lock: water gate on a canal or river.

116 *transfigured:* changed in appearance, usually to a more glorious state.

117 *husk:* empty shell.

chaps: jaws.

lax: loose, slack, careless.

degenerate: degraded, immoral.

A Time to Keep

120 *dresser:* kitchen sideboard with open shelves for dishes.

boozer: (slang) public house.

dominion: lordship.

reeked: smelt strongly.

parlour: old-fashioned sitting room for talking to guests.

Peveril of the Peak: one of Sir Walter Scott's worst novels.

extinguished: stopped burning, turned off.

121 *snapsack:* knapsack, canvas food-bag carried on the back.

pan: small coal shovel.

cobbles: small lumps of coal.

slack: coal-dust.

scullery: back kitchen for washing and dirty jobs.

nick: (slang) steal.

bracketed: propped up, sandwiched.

122 *daft:* (slang) crazy.

boisterous: cheerfully rough.

123 *'He worn't drug up':* he wasn't dragged up (brought up badly).

duck: dear.

yer: your.

Approved School: specially strict school for difficult children.

Detention Centre: short-stay prison for young offenders.

Borstal: prison for young criminals.

jocular: jokey, jolly.

half-inch: steal (rhyming slang for 'pinch').

sent down . . . for: imprisoned for (stealing).

Christmas box: present of money traditionally given to post, milk and dust men by householders at Christmas.

124 *avid:* keenly eager.

gob: (slang) mouth.

tar and concrete: building materials for roads.

shitting out motorway and coughing up signposts: Raymond's picture of his body as an efficient road-building machine is amusing but too crude for Martin's father.

wain't: won't.

head off: alter the direction of.

detected the manoeuvre: noticed the devious plan.

save face: keep his dignity.

censorious: critical.

looting . . . plundering: stealing in the manner often associated with conquering armies.

navvies: unskilled labourers.

gaffer: foreman.

125 *wok:* work.

bleeder: (slang) worthless person.

Nowt: nothing.

bleddy: bloody (used as a swear word).

Cut anybody's finger off who got too fresh: he would attack anyone who was rude to him.

chucked: (slang) thrown.

looney: mad.

'em: them.

summat: something.

quid: (slang) pound.

twigged: caught on, noticed.

the wind up: (slang) scared.

126 *wi':* with.

settle his hash: (slang) sort out his muddle, finish him off.

knackered: (slang) tired out.

wide: wide world.

our mam: mum, mother.

yer: you.

owt: anything.

scratch: standard.

owd banger: old noisy car.

ain't: aren't.

façade: ornamental front.

127 *mashing:* ingredients for making tea.

picture-house: old cinema.

battalion: large section of army.

mek: make.

Bastards will skin you dry, and fry you rotten: (slang) hateful tax-collectors will take all you have and make you suffer if they can.

128 *spongers:* (slang) parasites who live on other people.

Fuckers: (vulgar use) the fools.

trailer: caravan.

book myself in: clock on, sign to show I am here.

129 *livid:* purplish, throbbingly bright.

dumper truck: lorry with body that tilts to empty contents.

fucking: (vulgar use) wretched.

get the push: (slang) be sacked.

get my cards: lose my job.

compo: compensation money.

escarpment: steep slope.

mash-lad: tea-boy.

gone-out: (slang) puzzled.

burree din't say owt: but he didn't say anything.

beetling: quickly moving.

130 *bogger:* (vulgar use) bugger, miserable person.
    scoff: (slang) food.
    snout: (slang) tobacco.
    the clap: (slang) venereal disease.
131 *wafting:* waving.
    vivid: clear, bright.
    spoil bank: heap of dug-up earth.
    coin: earn in money.
    precipice: top of steep slope.
132 *piss off:* (vulgar use) go away.
    graft: (slang) hard work.
    sauntered: walked casually.
    lined: lined up along.
    pig-copper: (slang) swinish policeman.
    larking: fooling, playing.
133 *fags:* (slang) cigarettes.
    daft bastard: (slang) crazy idiot.
    Blokes: (slang) men.
    bleakly: coldly.
    bogger me if I did: (slang) I didn't at all.
    chokker: (slang) fellow.
    allus: always.
    any road up: in any case, anyway.
134 *tek:* take.
    tomorrer: tomorrow.
    mauler: rough hand.
    beer-off: off-licence, shop selling beer to take away.
    house: performance.

The Travellers

136 *wry:* grimly humorous.
    demeanour: behaviour to others.
    homburg: soft felt hat with narrow curled brim and high creased crown.

polka-dot: printed with a pattern of regular round spots.

spats: short gaiters which protect shoelaces and ankles.

expansiveness: broad swing.

137 *gimlet:* like a spike.

exponent of the three-card trick: person who shows racegoers how to play 'find the lady', where they bet on which of three cards is the Queen and always lose.

fleece: take money by fraud.

sentinels: guards.

band of black material: sign of mourning.

herring-bone tweed: rough-surfaced cloth with zigzag weave, very hard-wearing.

assent: agreement.

138 *flamboyant:* exaggerated.

peevishly: in a bad-tempered manner.

pitch: top.

nonplus: puzzle.

harangue: angry speech.

139 *telling:* impressive.

loco: locomotive, steam engine.

140 *'at:* that.

prostrate: lying down, exhausted.

teetotal: not an alcohol drinker.

141 *wa':* was.

budge him: make him give an inch, change his mind.

humoured him: let him have his own way.

'ud: would.

The Custodian

144 *incapacitation:* inability.

lurched: suddenly tilted.

145 *dunlin:* brown-backed sandpipers (birds).

causeway: raised road or footpath over or along low or wet ground.

146 *estuary:* river wide enough to have tides.

149 *whitebeam:* plant with white flowers, red berries and fuzzy-backed leaves.

152 *herons:* long-necked, long-legged, long-billed wading birds.

redshanks: wading birds with pale red legs and feet.

larks: small, brown, high-flying birds noted for their beautiful song.

dun: dusky grey-brown.

153 *curlew:* long-legged wader bird with long, thin, down-curving bill.

154 *beach:* sandy river-bank.

water mill: machine for grinding grain, powered by water-flow.

sail: set of boards on the arm of a windmill.

brackish: half-salt, half-fresh.

155 *fenland:* low-lying marshy area.

weird: supernatural, strange.

156 *plummeted:* fell like lead weights.

157 *creamy clots:* lumps like delicious thick (clotted) cream.

turquoise: the colour of a light greenish-blue gemstone.

gorse: prickly evergreen with yellow flowers.

leverets: young hares.

house martins: blue-black, white-bottomed, fork-tailed birds, type of swallow.

buzzard: type of hawk, larger but with rounder, shorter wings than a falcon.

copse: coppice, small group of trees left growing to supply timber occasionally.

158 *inevitable:* unavoidable.

alien: foreign.

159 *ingratiatingly sweet:* self-consciously trying to please.

160 *diversion:* retreat.

fumes: perfumes, fragrances.

night-jars: nocturnal swift-like birds, with 'churr' call, supposed to suck the milk of goats.

161 *pave:* prepare.

162 *cygnets:* young swans.

   peregrine: small, elegant, fast-flying falcon.

   distractedly: confusedly, agitatedly.

164 *lop off:* cut branches.

   thicket: shrubbery.

   frailty: fragility, weakness.

   rheumy: watery.

165 *runnels:* water channels.

   succumbed: gave in.

169 *imperceptibly:* unnoticeably.

170 *furtiveness:* guilty secrecy.

   hornets: large wasps with powerful stings.

   grubs: soft thick larvae of insects such as caterpillars and maggots.

   frowsty: un-aired, stuffy.

The authors: brief biographies

Mary Lavin

Mary Lavin is one of the four great writers of the modern Irish short story; the other three being Liam O'Flaherty, Frank O'Connor, and Sean O'Faolain. She is ten years younger than the youngest of them, and is still writing. Indeed a Penguin collection of her stories, representing each of her eleven volumes, was published only in 1981.

She was actually born in Massachusetts in the United States of America, but moved to Ireland when she was ten. She was educated in Ireland, and has lived there ever since. Her first husband was an Irish lawyer, and they had three daughters. After his death in 1959, she continued to live with her daughters on their farm in Bective, County Meath. Fifteen years later, she married an Australian, but they still live in the same farmhouse for part of the year and in Dublin for the rest.

Her first book of short stories, *Tales from Bective Bridge*, was published in 1942, and since then she has written well over a hundred stories, as she says: 'the work to which I have devoted myself almost exclusively for the past forty years.'

Mary Lavin always writes of Ireland; yet it is neither the closely and simply focused local concern of O'Flaherty, nor does she have the international stance of O'Connor or O'Faolain. She writes of all aspects of Irish life in stories deeply rooted in an acceptance of Ireland and its life, but making the particular of general interest and of wider importance. Often her theme is the role of women in the Irish life. Often she is critical of the pressures of life that control her characters, but always she writes with what the critic Walter Allen called 'a sense of fairness, dispassionateness, and discrimination in judgement similar to George Eliot's'. He sums up her achievement thus:

'It is one of Mary Lavin's excellences that she compels us through her stories to contemplate the difficulties of the moral life. As she shows us time and again, our good intentions are equalled only by our weaknesses. The theme implicit in her stories is the need for charity.'

Only recently has Mary Lavin had the wider recognition to equal the very high critical acclaim that she has always had. Writers in particular have always praised her; she has been awarded an honorary degree at her own old university (University College, Dublin), and the James Tait Black Memorial Prize. With each publication she received further praise, typical of which is the following from the novelist Anthony Burgess: 'I envy the skill of Mary Lavin . . . Her style is artfully flat. But in her capacity to make much out of little, to compress an entire ethos into an apparently banal situation, she reminds us of what literature is about.'

Her stories have been collected in three major volumes (Constable), but the easiest approach is through the Penguin selection: *Mary Lavin: Selected Stories*.

Nadine Gordimer

Nadine Gordimer was born in 1923 in a small town called Springs, on the string of gold mines that run east and west of Johannesburg, South Africa. Her father originally came from Lithuania, finally settling in Springs with a small jeweller's shop. Her childhood, she says, was very strange and lonely. From the age of nine, she no longer attended school as she suffered from a heart complaint. She dates the beginning of her writing from this time. The society she grew up in was made up of immigrants who ran the stores and their customers, the mine workers who had themselves been uprooted from their homelands in Africa. Both sides were bewildered by their strange environment, 'so the relationships tended to be rough, people shouting at each other, and I noticed this as a child' remembers Nadine Gordimer. 'When I was in late adolescence, I began to see that this was an amazing situation. I was beginning to think about the position of whites in South Africa, the strangeness of their being there, and also beginning to look at those black workers – there had been thousands around me all my life, since I was born – and seeing them as people.'

In eight novels and seven collections of short stories, Nadine Gordimer has won international acclaim for her sharp-edged portrayals of South African life under apartheid. In 1974 she was joint winner of the Booker McConnell Prize for her novel *The Conservationist*, in 1961 *Friday's Footprint* won the W. H. Smith Award, and the James Tait Black Memorial Prize was awarded to *A Guest of Honour* in 1972. The Scottish Arts Council made her the fifth Neil Gunn International Fellow, a tribute to novelists of international distinction and achievement. Her latest novel *July's People* has much to offer readers who have enjoyed her short stories. It is a fictional account of a white, middle-class family fleeing into the bush to escape a black revolution, but as with much of Nadine Gordimer's work, it moves from a particular situation into its universal implication: here a sort of apocalyptic vision.

Nadine Gordimer is often called a political writer. In an interview with *Newsweek* in 1982 she said:

> My intention is not to be political, but South African life is so saturated with political meanings. It's rather like the Soviet Union or Poland. If you're writing honestly about your society, and that society is in turmoil, you become a political writer.

Nadine Gordimer's work has evolved from a literary tradition that was South African to one that she has called 'an African-centred consciousness'. Another novel, *Burger's Daughter*, reflects this change as it illustrates the way in which black activists have been ignored while white South African activists attract world attention. She feels there is a basic cultural link between people

195

in a continent, and in an interview for the *London Magazine* in 1983, explained

> that there is something that comes through from the earth itself in each continent. And I think that even if you are white, if you were born in Africa and you have rejected both consciously and subconsciously the colonial consciousness, if you are not just floating on the surface of the society in which you live and ignoring its true entities which are the over-whelming presence of black people – if you don't ignore this then you too share in the real sense of Africa, the human sense of Africa and the physical sense of the land. It enters into your work through your perceptions. Where do writers get their earliest perceptions? They come from the quality of the light, the kind of mud you play with, the kind of trees you climb. Well I am white, but those trees and that mud were Africa, so they are inside me and they come out, I suppose, in one's work. . . .
>
> I feel inadequate as a human being in my situation as a white South African but as a writer I think I have arrived at a stage through my work where if I write about blacks or I create black characters, I feel I have the right to do so. I know enough to do so. I accept the limitations of what I know.

All of Nadine Gordimer's works have been banned in South Africa.

V. S. Naipaul

Of the many fascinating short-story writers who grew up in the West Indies, V. S. Naipaul has established the widest reputation throughout the world. His family was one of the many who came from India as 'indentured labourers' a hundred years ago. After the abolition of slavery, the sugar cane and coconut growers of the plantations of the West Indies looked around the world for cheap laboureres to replace the lost slaves. After trying poor workers from many countries, it was to India that colonial England looked for these workers. Under Government regulation and carefully controlled wages and conditions, they and their familes were shipped across the world to start new lives in the West Indies. V. S. Naipaul's grandfather came in this way to Trinidad, and with other indentured labourers living in 'barracks' created an Indian community. This 'small and remote community', as Naipaul called it in his book *India: a Wounded Civilisation*, retained its religion, customs, and style of family life, and today is still recognizably a somewhat different part of the community in Trinidad. As he says: 'The customs of my childhood were somewhat mysterious' – they had been transported around the world, and were carefully preserved even if their reasons were no longer fully known.

For the young Naipaul, the India of his grandfather was 'a country never physically described and therefore never real, a country out in the void beyond the dot of Trinidad; and from it our journey had been final' (as he says in another book *An Area of Darkness*). However, he was very aware of the distant and lost India:

More than in people, India lay about us in things: in a string bed or two, grimy, tattered, no longer serving any function, never repaired because there was no one with this caste skill in Trinidad, yet still permitted to take up room; in plaited straw mats; in innumerable brass vessels; in wooden printing blocks, never used because printed cotton was abundant and cheap and because the secret of the dyes had been forgotten, no dyer being at hand; in books, the sheets large, coarse and brittle, the ink thick and oily; in drums and one ruined harmonium; in brightly coloured pictures of deities on pink lotus or radiant against Himalayan snow; and in all the paraphernalia of the prayer-room: the brass bells and gongs and camphor-burners like Roman lamps, the slender-handled spoon for the doling out of the consecrated 'nectar'

197

(peasant's nectar: on ordinary days brown sugar and water, with some shreds of the tulsi leaf, sweetened milk on high days), the images, the smooth pebbles, the stick of sandalwood.

Naipaul was born in 1932, and went to a secondary school that was thought of as particularly good, Queen's Royal College. In 1950 he came to England to do a university course at Oxford, and soon after began to write. From the beginning, his books were popular and well thought of. His first was *The Mystic Masseur*, published in 1957 and winning the John Llewellyn Rhys Memorial Prize. After *The Suffrage of Elvira* in 1958, he published his first collection of short stories the following year: *Miguel Street*. This also won a prize (the Somerset Maugham Award).It is a collection based on the characters associated with a particular street in Trinidad, and many of the stories are very funny as well as being perceptive and having a meaning beyond the particular circumstances described.

He continued to live in England, though he re-visited the West Indies. His books continued to win prizes, and were widely read. In 1967 his second collection of short stories, from which *The Heart* in this collection has been taken, was published. *The Loss of El Dorado* (1969), *In a Free State* (1971, and winner of the Booker Prize), and *Guerrillas* (1975) were his next books.

From about 1960 he started travelling, especially to India, from where his ancestors had come. Three books came from these travels: *The Middle Passage* (1962), an impression of colonial society, *An Area of Darkness*, an autobiographical study (1964), and *India: A Wounded Civilisation* (1977).

He is considered by many people to be 'the finest living novelist in English', and everything he writes is interesting, disturbing, often comic, and very sensitive.

Doris Lessing

Doris Lessing was born in Persia in 1919. At the age of six, she went with her parents to Southern Rhodesia where her father became a farmer. She returned to England when she was thirty and has lived here ever since.

She wrote her first novel *The Grass is Singing* while still living in Southern Rhodesia, now called Zimbabwe, and has since written over a dozen celebrated novels and half a dozen volumes of short stories.

Much of her work is set in Africa and reflects her concern with relations between people, especially between black and white on that continent. In 1967, she wrote in an introduction to a Longman Imprint collection of her stories:

> Novels, stories, plays can convey the truth about personal relations, emotions, and attitudes of which the people subject to them are perhaps unaware, or only partly aware: literature comes out of atmospheres, climates of opinion, everything that can not be described by the economic, the sociological approaches. You can read a hundred factual books or surveys about a country, or, for that matter, a factory or a farm, and you'll learn nothing of what a person experiencing that country, that factory, or farm feels or thinks.

As many of her African short stories in particular are written from the point of view of a young person, it is tempting to interpret her work autobiographically, but further on in that same introduction, she explains:

> None of these stories is 'true' in the sense that things happened exactly as I've written them. Those of you who are learning to write stories will have found, perhaps, that the way to do it is to let yourself be attracted by an incident, an overheard remark, a face; and then allow this germ to grow,

to accumulate around it memories, associations, things of a similar substance, until a whole is reached with a shape, a texture of its own, and very different from how it started off. If you describe something direct – that's reportage, journalism. Good journalism is fidelity to the fact and needs its own kind of discipline. What makes a story is the passivity, learning to wait, allowing the slow simmering process to take place – patience. For me, as for many other white people who lived in Africa, what accumulates and grows is the feeling of Africa itself, the love of the place.

Alongside her interest in racial relations Doris Lessing is known for her writing about modern woman. When asked in a television interview how she felt to be called 'the first feminist writer' she denied this term, feeling she has responded to a 'general consciousness'. Nevertheless her five-volume novel sequence *Children of Violence*, and novels like *The Golden Notebook* eloquently present the developing role of women, their passions and anxieties, since the war.

Doris Lessing's vision extends to the future in a series of novels with the title of *Canopus in Argos: Archives*. Another so-called science fiction is *Memoirs of a Survivor*, which has recently been filmed.

Dan Jacobson

Dan Jacobson was born in Johannesburg in 1929 of Jewish immigrant parents from Lithuania. In 1954 he came to England. He says of this time:

> I thought I'd get a job of some kind, but I found that I was able to make enough by freelance writing, so I just carried on doing so. Quite a lot of my income arrived in unexpected ways – not directly from the sales of books. Some came through movie and drama options from which movies and

dramas were never made. But a short story, improbably enough, was turned into a musical which had a fairly successful run on Broadway. *The Zulu and the Zayda* it was called. I went to the States and put in time as a creative writing person. In those days one could make enough both to cover one's living there and bring home money when one returned to this country. I did quite a lot of literary journalism; and produced short stories fairly steadily. Contrary to what people say, they were a good way of earning money, provided the stories were sold to magazines in the United States. That was absolutely essential. Then they could be sold again here, and put in a collection, and so forth. Unfortunately I haven't written any stories for a long time now. Anyway, such money as I made came from many different directions. But inflation blew most of it away; plus the fact that I now write more slowly than I used to. I found I wasn't making ends meet.

So, he became a lecturer in English Literature at University College, London.

Dan Jacobson's novels include *The Trap, A Dance in the Sun, The Price of Diamonds, The Evidence of Love, The Beginners, The Rape of Tamar, The Wonder-Worker* and most recently published, *The Confessions of Josef Baisz.* He has also published a travel book on the United States, *No Further West* and a book of short stories called *A Long Way From London,* for which he won the John Rhys Memorial Prize. He has said that only a few of his stories were written before he came to England, and, in terms of publication, his work is wholly English. But he says, 'Most of what I've written has been set in South Africa – quantitatively, in numbers of words. My own feeling, though, is that I've gone round the course twice as a novelist: first as a South African writer; then, more recently, over the last seven or eight years, writing fiction which is not only not about South Africa, but is also a different kind of fiction from what had gone before.' He explains:

If I became a writer for any single reason, it was that I loved reading as a kid; and I didn't love it because it was an educative or morally improving activity, but because it was a way of being other than I was, someone else. For as long as the book lasted, there I was, part of the Biggles saga, or the *Boy's Own Paper*, or whatever else I was reading. And as I grew older this was still essentially the reason why I loved reading and wanted to become a writer. I wanted to participate in this activity, this other-making activity. And I have always hoped that the books I write are enjoyable, that they are fun, they are exciting. At the same time, looking back, I do now feel that when I was writing about South Africa I was responding to certain quasi-moral obligations, external to me, which I could not avoid. However, when I found that I no longer wished to write about South Africa, or rather that I could no longer write about South Africa, I felt liberated because I was no longer working under those external obligations. For example, when I wrote *The Rape of Tamar* I was the only one in the world who knew what it was like in the court of King David three thousand years ago. It was just as I described it. It had to be. It's the same with the Republic of Sarmeda in *The Confessions of Josef Baisz*. I've made it all up. I'm the authority on Sarmeda. Therefore, I'm free to say as little or as much about particular aspects of it as I wish.

Dan Jacobson's writing is noted for its unusual sensitivity, especially in drawing out the implications in an anecdote on which a story has been based. He says of his writing:

I think I see the settings before I see the characters, in a curious way. Or I see particular moods which belong inextricably with particular settings rather than characters. Books seem to me to emerge more out of moods than out of characters.

Like every writer, he is often asked if his characters are modelled on real people. He says he finds this question difficult to answer:

> I simply don't know. Also you must not forget that if you take a so-called real character and put him in an imaginary situation, he is then transformed. If I take somebody, a schoolteacher for instance, who I can remember from when I was twelve, and turn him into a Polar explorer in one of my short stories, it is no longer the same schoolteacher that I can remember from twelve years old. That kind of transformation can take place in fiction.

Readers of this volume, might enjoy others of Dan Jacobson's short stories in the volumes *Through the Wilderness* and *A Way of Life and Other Stories*.

Angus Wilson

Angus Wilson was born in 1913 in Bexhill, Sussex, and worked as Assistant Keeper in the Department of Printed Books at the British Museum before being seconded to the Foreign Office during the war. He was appointed Professor of English Literature at the University of East Anglia in 1966. He says of himself:

> I didn't start writing until I was 39. I wrote short stories, because I only had weekends to write in, and I couldn't write anything long. I had to learn to write novels.

Angus Wilson's best-known works are *Anglo-Saxon Attitudes*, *Such Darling Dodos*, *Hemlock and After*, *The Middle Age of Mrs Eliot*, which won the James Tait Black Memorial Prize, and *Setting the World on Fire*. In his novels, Wilson's moral preoccupation has been with the collapse of liberalism in our time, a view that derives from his emotionally less intense but intellectually far more stimulating contacts with people after his mother's death who became for him a kind of substitute family. By contrast, the short story, he believes, can make do solely with the other requisites for fiction: an ear for dialogue, an eye for description, and a sense of drama, or conflict. In fact, Wilson's stories often reveal a definite, mature point of view, while his novels contain much more 'that must be meditated, that must be thought about intellectually – thought about hard'. He insists that no matter how serious his intellectual preoccupation may be, the writer must quickly 'go back and recharge all that with life and with drama' if his novel is to be any good.

Speaking of his personal experience, Wilson says 'It seems to me that I am at once a more impulsive, a more bitchy, and a more compassionate author . . . that my humanism has less high hope for the future but more acceptance of liking human beings as they are.' He says that he is trying to resolve a conflict between his own liberal and humane attitude towards life and certain deep-seated cruel instincts. His father was an aggressive man, who loved the sight of blood, whether of human beings or fighting animals. He once told his son how, on a journey back from a rendezvous with his mistress in St John's Wood, he picked a fight with an innocent passer-by. He was a gambler, and the family lived a peripatetic life in hotels, on a declining income from rented property. His wife suffered his philanderings for years, though the couple were always parting. Happiness was fleeting and precarious for the young Wilson.

His mother died suddenly when he was 15. His father's death some years later hardly affected him as much. Nor did the experience of returning home from London one Saturday afternoon to discover his landlady, whom he much enjoyed living with, lying on the floor in a paralytic seizure. 'I have written about the death of that old woman in three different forms in my writing,' he says. 'I have also written about somebody dying in a hotel, but I've made it my father and never my mother.' Not only has he refused to discard or renounce childish things, he cherishes his child-like awarenesses, perceptions and intuitions. 'To do this is limited and dangerous, but not if you're aware you're doing it, and also keep your adult sense,' he says. A 'strange transport' between adult and child is what he terms the process by which he lives.

Apart from his fiction, Wilson has written much acclaimed studies of Dickens (*The World of Charles Dickens*) and Kipling (*The Strange Ride of Rudyard Kipling*).

V. S. Pritchett

Sir Victor Sawdon Pritchett was born in Ipswich, Suffolk, in 1900 and spent most of his early days on the move, as the eldest child of a Yorkshireman who 'walked in and out of jobs with the bumptiousness of a god'. His father was a devout Christian Scientist and readers of Pritchett's short stories will often find there a puritan figure from the lower middle classes, who resembles his father. One consequence of his parents' poverty was that they could not afford to maintain him at Alleyn's, his 'excellent' London grammar school, beyond the age of fifteen. He was put to work in the leather trade.

> I've always been an outsider. Writers ought not to have it too easy. They oughtn't to be too privileged. My background gave me a much more various view of English society than if I'd followed the proper tramlines, and as such was very enriching. Another good thing was that I didn't have the educated Englishman's rather patronizing view of foreigners – their funny clothes, their odd behaviour. And that was an advantage when I came to write about them.

His most popular books include the two volumes about his youth: *A Cab at the Door* and *Midnight Oil*.

By the age of twenty, Pritchett knew he wanted to become a writer and, like many other optimistic apprentice artists, he set off with £20 to Paris and worked in a photographer's shop. Not knowing what to write about, he began by describing his room and the groans of the landlady next door. He sold the sketch to the Christian Science Monitor. *The Monitor* liked his sketches and in due course sent him to Ireland and then Spain as their correspondent. Spain gave him his first book, a travel book called *Marching Spain*, and his first successful short story, *The Spanish Virgin*. He wrote his first novel at the same time (of the five he altogether produced, he considered only one of his novels, *Deadman Leading*, any good!). Short-story writing remained throughout his life his first love.

He compared writing short stories to composing a sonnet, both requiring discipline, harmony and economy. For every page he kept, as many as six were thrown away – 'Particularly when you're starting – that's the most important thing in writing a short story: getting the right start. And by right start I don't necessarily mean an event, but setting the right note. It's as though one were hearing a song, getting the key of the song right. And it's very rarely that one gets that right straight-away.' Pritchett also said that 'Explanation is the great Vice'. You must, he believed, show things as they happen – 'and not, after you've done so, or in the course of doing so, explain why they've happened in this way. It's rather like a conjuror doing a trick but at the same time doing it in slow motion and explaining how he does it. That is scientifically interesting but as a form of magic is hopeless.'

He does not write for the reader, either.

People are always rather shocked to hear that, particularly if they enjoy reading my stuff. I say No, I don't write for you at all. I write for myself, in order to find out what I think. If I wrote for the reader I would be trying to imagine what you want. My mind is a frightful muddle of impressions, sensations and thoughts. I must sort this out, and I'm rather inclined to do it from the writer's point of view.

He said that he was a visual artist, having once hoped to paint. 'I haven't a literal eye, but seeing images is strong in me.' At the same time, his prose is uncannily close to the spoken word. He liked the sounds of people's speech, and the contradictions that lie between what they say and the drama of their lives. Readers of this volume will find a similar comedy to *The Saint* in the short stories, *It May Never Happen*, *The Sailor* and *Aunt Gertrude*.

In the 'Thirties, Pritchett joined the reviewing staff of the *New Statesman*, mainly to finance his short-story writing, and became its leading light, writer of the 'Books in General' column, which he devoted, during the war, to reassessing the classics. His pieces were addictive to people starved of literature. For this he was paid a princely £5 a column. He and his wife Dorothy could not afford to live in London. They rented a Georgian farmhouse in the Lambourn valley, Berkshire, at £1 a week, with no light, heat or mains water. Pritchett talks of himself as an 'amateur' critic, but many authors still consider him Britain's most human and intelligent critic.

Alan Sillitoe

Alan Sillitoe was born in Nottingham, England, in 1928 and says that 'until I was nineteen, I didn't think of writing at all. I was just having a good time like any other young man; I was working in a factory and spending my money.'

He worked in the Raleigh Bicycle Factory in Coventry, where his father also worked, until he was called up to join the RAF at eighteen. He had to leave the airforce because of tuberculosis, and spent eighteen months in hospital.

Before then I had hardly read any 'adult' books, but during my enforced retirement from life, and to absorb the shock of it, I read hundreds. During this time I also began to write,

207

mostly poems, but one or two short stories. At twenty-one I wrote my first novel. In seventeen days I wrote the whole hundred thousand words of it. It was some years before I was able to see how bad it was.

After leaving hospital Alan Sillitoe lived on Majorca for a time, doing odd jobs, and writing a number of short stories and incidents about a young man in Nottingham. Eventually these were to become his first published novel, *Saturday Night and Sunday Morning*, which won a prize for the best novel in 1958, and soon became a successful film.

Because he left school early, he says he first lacked the confidence to write about his own life, 'working class in the 1930s':

A big question I often ask myself is why I didn't write *Saturday Night and Sunday Morning* when I was twenty-two, say, or twenty-three, but I couldn't do this because all the earlier novels were mostly about fantasies or they were pastiches of other writers, like Lawrence and Dostoyevsky; they were, shall we say, in a middle-class world, and it took me a long time to get out of that and begin to feel my own feet, and know that what I should write about was the life I knew in Nottingham which was the most vivid to me.

Nottingham boys feature in many of his short stories, like *The Ragman's Daughter* and *The Loneliness of the Long-Distance Runner*. Readers who enjoyed these and the short story in this volume, might also enjoy the story of another Nottingham boy, in Sillitoe's novel *Key to the Door*.

Stan Barstow

Stan Barstow was born in 1928, the only child of a coal miner, in what was then called the West Riding of Yorkshire, in

Northern England. He began his working life in the drawing office of a local engineering firm. He remembers:

At this time in my early twenties I got an awful feeling that I'd somehow taken a wrong turning in life. I was an engineering draughtsman and had a good job by all the standards I knew; but it was one which left me feeling curiously dissatisfied with my lot and not at all ambitious to advance in that field. This frustration led me to look for a creative hobby and to the daring thought that many of the stories I read in magazines weren't very good and, with a bit of practice, I ought to be able to do as well. I was not really writing for money: it never occurred to me that I had anything serious to say or that anyone might take me seriously. That came later when I found that writing insincerely rarely works, and realized that what I ought to be writing about was the kind of working-class life I knew from my own experience.

But he found that at that time stories with regional working-class settings were not as popular as they are today, and it was not until *A Kind of Loving* which was a Book Society Choice in 1960 and then a successful film that he was able to take up writing full time.

When a first collection of stories, *The Desperadoes*, was published in 1961, many had already been broadcast by the BBC. Stan Barstow still writes for radio, television, magazines and the theatre. He says about television writing:

There is in it a serious drawback for a writer of my temperament, and this is that most television plays are shown once and then forgotten. I have always had a passion for the permanent nature of the written word and, though television wasn't nationwide when I first started to write, back in the early nineteen fifties, I think, even if it had been I should still have become primarily a prose-fiction writer.

His early novels might be of particular interest to readers of this volume: *Ask Me Tomorrow* (1962), *Joby* (1964), and *The Watchers on the Shore* (1966).

Susan Hill

Susan Hill was born in 1942 in Scarborough, Yorkshire, and studied English at King's College, London, before joining the *Coventry Evening Telegraph* as a book critic. 'It was,' she says, 'very good, the old professional training, being told to write 800 words by Wednesday. But it was pretty soul destroying. You spent an awful lot of time reading bad novels.' She gave up her job after five years, determined to earn her living by writing. 'I had to take the plunge and write on my own. I starved for a year or so, but it was all right after that.'

Her first novel had been published while she was still at school, her second, while she was in her final year at college – 'They were pretty bad – they're happily out of print now.' But her later efforts met with more lasting success. *I'm the King of the Castle*, published in 1970, won her the Somerset Maugham Award for young writers. *The Albatross*, a collection of short stories, won her the John Llewellyn Rhys prize, and the *Bird of Night*, the Whitbread Award. Her last novel, *In the Springtime of the Year*, published in 1974, was the fictionalized account of her own grief at the sudden, early death of an intimate friend. That, too, was a bestseller.

Since then she has concentrated on literary journalism and radio plays. The change, after more than a decade of concentrated novel writing, surprised many people. But the reason, according to Susan Hill herself, was that she simply ran out of steam. Happily married and with a daughter to look after, she said she simply did not have the spare emotional energy to write novels – 'tearing bits out of yourself and putting them into a book.' She still had plenty of ideas, but not ones that she wanted to turn into novels or short stories.

It just happened that way. But I like writing radio plays very much, and I shall go on doing that. At the moment, with very limited working time, I tend to write things that need short bursts of time. Curiously enough, I can write plays in short bursts and then come back to them the next day, which I couldn't do with novels.

She has also written regularly about books and writers for *The Daily Telegraph*, and been a regular appearer on book programmes on radio and television.

In 1982, *The Magic Apple Tree* was published to critical acclaim. A gentle book about the effects of the changing seasons on the English countryside and community. With a marvellous sense of the interdependence and simple kindness experienced in village life, it is a book that readers of this volume might well enjoy.

Further reading

The scope for reading modern short stories is immense. This selected reading list has been compiled for the senior examination student. Collections by all the authors represented in this volume are included. There are also a number of other key recent authors, and a small collection of anthologies. All have been chosen with student needs in mind.

Selected authors

MICHAEL ANTHONY   *Cricket on the Road*, Heinemann Caribbean Writers (1973).

STAN BARSTOW   *A Casual Acquaintance and Other Stories*, edited by Marilyn Davies, Longman Imprint Books (1976).
The Human Element, edited by Marilyn Davies, Longman Imprint Books (1970).

H. E. BATES   *The Good Corn and Other Stories*, edited by Geoffrey Halson, Longman Imprint Books (1974).

ELIZABETH BOWEN   *Collected Stories*, Cape (1981).

SID CHAPLIN   *The Leaping Lad And Other Stories*, edited by Geoffrey Halson, Longman Imprint Books (1970).

BRIAN FRIEL   *A Saucer of Larks*, Faber (1962). Out of print.

NADINE GORDIMER   *Livingstone's Companions*, Cape (1972).
A Soldier's Embrace, Cape (1975).
Selected Stories, Cape (1975).
Six Feet in the Country, Cape (1956). Out of print.
Some Monday for Sure, Heinemann African Writers (1976).

SUSAN HILL   *A Bit of Singing and Dancing*, Hamish Hamilton (1973).
The Albatross and Other Stories, Penguin (1974).

CHRISTOPHER ISHERWOOD   *An Isherwood Selection*, edited by Geoffrey Halson, Longman Imprint Books (1979).

DAN JACOBSON *A Way of Life and Other Stories*, Longman Imprint Books. Out of print.

Beggar My Neighbour, Short Stories, Secker and Warburg (1963). Out of print.

The Trap and a Dance in the Sun, Secker and Warburg (1980).

RUTH PRAWER JHABVALA *How I Became a Holy Mother and Other Stories*, Penguin (1981).

Like Birds, Like Fishes and Other Stories, John Murray (1963).

MARY LAVIN *Selected Stories*, Penguin (1981).

DORIS LESSING *Collected African Stories*, Michael Joseph (1973), in two volumes:

This Was the Old Chief's Country and *Sun Between Their Feet*.

Collected Stories, Cape (1978), in two volumes: *To Room Nineteen* and *Temptation of Jack Orkney*.

Nine African Stories, edited by Michael Marland, Longman Imprint Books (1968).

MICHAEL MCLAVERTY *Collected Short Stories*, Poolbeg Press (1979).

V. S. NAIPAUL *Miguel Street*, Heinemann Caribbean Writers (1975).

A Flag on the Island, Penguin (1969).

BILL NAUGHTON *Late Night on Watling Street*, edited by Graham Owens, Longman Imprint Books (1969).

EDNA O'BRIEN *A Scandalous Woman and Other Stories*, Penguin (1976).

The Love Object, Penguin (1970).

FRANK O'CONNOR *Day Dreams and Other Stories*, Pan Books (1973).

Mad Lomasneys and Other Stories, Pan Books (1970).

My Oedipus Complex and Other Stories, Penguin (1970).

The Holy Door and Other Stories, Pan Books (1973).

SEAN O'FAOLAIN *Collected Stories*, Constable (1980).

Foreign Affairs and Other Stories, Constable (1976).

Selected Stories, Constable (1978).

LIAM O'FLAHERTY *Pedlar's Revenge and Other Stories*, edited by Angeline Kelly, Wolfhound Press (1976).

213

Short Stories, New English Library, in two volumes: I (1970) and II (1981).

V. S. PRITCHETT *On the Edge of the Cliff and Other Stories*, Chatto and Windus (1980).

Selected Stories, Chatto and Windus (1978).

FRANK SARGESON *Collected Stories, 1935–1963*, Martin Brian and O'Keefe (1965). Out of print.

SAMUEL SELVON *Ways of Sunlight*, edited by J. Grant, Longman Caribbean (1979).

ALAN SILLITOE *A Sillitoe Selection*, edited by Michael Marland, Longman Imprint Books (1968).

The Ragman's Daughter, Star Books (1977).

Saturday Night and Sunday Morning, Star Books (1975).

The Second Chance, Cape (1981).

GILLIAN TINDALL *Dances of Death*, Hodder and Stoughton. Out of print.

JOHN WAIN *A John Wain Selection*, edited by Geoffrey Halson, Longman Imprint Books (1977).

The Lifeguard, Macmillan. Out of print.

ANGUS WILSON *A Bit off the Map*, Secker and Warburg (1956).

Such Darling Dodos, Panther (1980).

The Wrong Set and Other Stories, Panther (1982).

Selected collections

ALFRED BRADLEY and KAY JAMIESON *Dandelion Clocks: Stories of Childhood*, Penguin (1980).

NANCY DEAN and MYRA STARK *In the Looking Glass, Twenty-one Modern Short Stories by Women*, Putnam and Sons, New York. Out of print.

CECIL GRAY *Images, Caribbean Short Stories*, Nelson (1973).

MICHAEL MARLAND (ed.) *Caribbean Stories*, Longman Imprint Books (1978).

The Experience of Love, Longman Imprint Books (1980).

Loves, Hopes and Fears, Longman Imprint Books (1975).

Meetings and Partings, Longman Imprint Books (to be published in 1984).

ANNA RUTHERFORD and HANNAH DONALD (eds), *Commonwealth Short Stories*, Macmillan (1979).

ANDREW SALKEY (ed.) *West Indian Stories*, Faber (1968).

Acknowledgements

We are grateful to the following for permission to reproduce short stories:

the author's agents for 'The Travellers' by Stan Barstow from *A Season with Eros* pub. Michael Joseph Ltd; Jonathan Cape Ltd for 'A Time to Keep' by Alan Sillitoe from *The Second Chance*; Chatto & Windus Ltd for 'The Saint' by V. S. Pritchett from *Collected Stories*, 1982; Constable & Co Ltd for 'The Patriot Son' by Mary Lavin from *Collected Stories*; the author's agents for 'Country Lovers' by Nadine Gordimer from *Six Feet of the Country* pub. Jonathan Cape Ltd, © Nadine Gordimer 1975; the author's agents for 'The Custodian' by Susan Hill from *A Bit of Singing & Dancing* pub. Hamish Hamilton 1975; the author's agents for 'The Boss' by Dan Jacobson from *The Evidence of Love* pub. Weidenfeld & Nicolson; the author's agents for 'The Second Hut' by Doris Lessing from *This was the Old Chief's Country*, © Doris Lessing 1951; the author's agent for 'The Heart' by V. S. Naipaul from *A Flag on the Island* © V. S. Naipaul 1967; Martin Secker & Warburg Ltd for 'Raspberry Jam' by Angus Wilson from *The Wrong Set*, 1949.

Study questions

1 *The Patriot Son* by Mary Lavin
What aspects of the patriotic movement does Matty find attractive, and what aspects are like faery lights 'to lure men to folly and destruction'?

2 *Country Lovers* by Nadine Gordimer
Paulus says, 'I feel like killing myself.' Thebedi says, 'It was a thing of our childhood.' Explain as fully as possible what they mean by these statements, and why Paulus feels it necessary to kill his baby daughter.

3 *The Heart* by V. S. Naipaul
The thing that Hari feared 'more than anything' happens, just after his 'triumph'. How far does Hari deserve to lose his dog? Consider his age, his physical condition, his social situation at school and his emotional reasons for treating the dog as he does. Consider also his mother's attitude towards him and his pet, his father's actions in the story, and their wisdom in giving Hari an Alsatian puppy.

4 *The Second Hut* by Doris Lessing
Compare and contrast the characters of Major Carruthers and Van Heerden. Consider their attitudes to the country and its people, to their wives and children, and to each other. How satisfactory do you find the ending in the light of this comparison and contrast?

5 *The Boss* by Dan Jacobson
'"Everything begins, and everything ends, sooner or later."
"No, Mr Kramer," Miss Posen said, daring to insist.
And as a reward he gave her a lift home that evening.'
Why does Miss Posen dare to insist on defying her new boss, and why should Mr Kramer want to 'reward' her? How 'right' is Lionel to spy on Miss Posen, and what 'fight' does Mr Kramer know has been won at the end?

6 *Raspberry Jam* by Angus Wilson
Mr Codrington says: 'No, let us retain the fantasies, the imag-

inative games of childhood, even at the expense of a little fear, for they are the true magnificence of the springtime of life.' What fantasies and imaginative games do the Swindale sisters retain in the autumn of their lives, and what problems does this clinging to the past bring them? How far are Johnnie's fantasies and games 'magnificient', and how far is his mother right to suspect they may be 'very bad for him', and his father to be upset and beat him?

7 *The Saint* by V. S. Pritchett

The narrator compares Mr Timberlake to a Greek statue of a god, a pillow, a fizzy liquid, a decorated saint, a real saint, and a husk. He compares his own religious doubt to an ape. Show how Pritchett gradually develops and combines these images through the story, and brings them all together in the final sentence.

8 *A Time to Keep* by Alan Sillitoe

What aspects of work as 'a place of pay and violence which his father detested' does Martin discover during his day with his cousin? What do you understand by the title?

9 *The Travellers* by Stan Barstow

For what reasons is the old man's daughter so angry, and what do they tell us about her attitude to her father and step-mother? How do you understand the narrator's 'No' at the end?

10 *The Custodian* by Susan Hill

In July, Mr Bowry thinks he should have said, 'Take him away, take him away now,' when Blaydon arrived in April. Explain why he thinks this, and explain why Blaydon judges it best to leave when he does. Why do you think Blaydon does not warn Mr Bowry, or tell him where and how the boy is?

Select and describe some of the ways in which the countryside and its changing seasons play an important part in this story.

11 What do you learn about South Africa and its mixed population from *The Second Hut*? How helpful are events like these, set in 1931, to your understanding of the present situation in South Africa?

12 How far does reading *The Patriot Son* help you to understand the continuing problems in Northern Ireland?

13 What similarities and what differences do you find between Nadine Gordimer's portrayal of life in South Africa and Doris Lessing's?

14 In what ways are the stories of *Raspberry Jam* and *A Time to Keep* similar?

15 Compare Mr Kramer's attitude to his son in *The Boss* with that of Matty's mother to hers in *The Patriot Son*.

16a Compare the differing ways in which Angus Wilson and Susan Hill use the sudden death of a bird as the turning point in their stories.

b Compare the differing ways in which Doris Lessing and Nadine Gordimer use the sudden death of a baby as the turning point of their stories.

c Consider the differing attitudes to the death of an adult shown by Stan Barstow, Alan Sillitoe and V. S. Pritchett in their stories.

In each case you should discuss how the death affects the structure of the plot, the development of the characters, and the emotional effect which the author wishes to have on the reader.

17 'A first reading makes you want to know what will happen; a second makes you understand why it happens; a third makes you think.'

How true is this statement of any two or three stories in this selection? Examine what methods the authors use to make the reader wonder what will happen.

18 'There are no clear divisions between good and evil, nor between comedy and tragedy: but then people and life are like that.'

Select two or three stories and show how the authors present characters with both good and bad, weak and strong points; and show how they enable us to smile and see the humorous side while still presenting essentially sad subjects such as death, parting, failure and loneliness.